D0984014

THE CRUISER

BARTOLOMEO COLLEONI

Anatomy
of the
Ship

THE CRUISER

BARTOLOMEO COLLEONI

Franco Gay & Valerio Gay

Naval
Institute
Press

First published in Great Britain 1987 by
Conway Maritime Press Ltd
24 Bride Lane, Fleet Street,
London EC4Y 8DR

Published and distributed in the United
States of America and Canada by the Naval
Institute Press, Annapolis, Maryland 21402

Library of Congress Catalog Card No
87-61493

ISBN 0-87021-900-6

This edition is authorized for sale only in the
United States and its territories and
possession, and Canada

Manufactured in Great Britain

Contents

INTRODUCTION

The origins of the light cruiser can be traced back to the 'protected cruiser' of the late nineteenth century. These vessels eschewed side armour in favour of a protective deck at about waterline level over the machinery and other vital spaces, and although they tended to be smaller than the armoured cruiser, there were examples of very large protected cruisers, like the British *Powerful* and *Terrible* at 14,000 tons. Simultaneously, much smaller cruisers were being developed for use as fleet scouts and leaders of destroyer flotillas and at first these vessels had some deck protection but later classes adopted limited side armour as well.

The British and Germans built large numbers of this type of 'light armoured' cruiser from about 1910 to the end of the First World War. War experience tended to standardise the main armament of this type as 6in (or 5.9in for the German navy). Other navies had less use for light cruisers, Italy for example possessing only three small 'esploratori' (scouts) in 1914.

After the war Italy became increasingly wary of French Mediterranean ambitions, and was concerned at the Washington naval conference to obtain parity with France. However, as far as its provisions applied to cruisers the Washington treaty limited construction to ships of no more than 10,000 tons and 8in (203mm) guns. These heavy or 'Treaty' cruisers were built in some numbers by all the major powers, but there were also smaller ships which the 1930 London conference defined as 'light' cruisers with no more than 6in (152mm) guns. Although France and Italy were not signatories of this treaty, they were both to build ships which could be described as light cruisers.

In the immediate post-war period Italy had added to her modest group of three 'esploratori' two ex-Austro-Hungarian scouts and three ex-German light cruisers which had been assigned as war reparations. The two ex-Austro-Hungarian units, severly battle-worn, were of no great value; the three ex-German cruisers were better; they were still in good condition although they must have taken quite an active part in the war. In terms of usefulness to the Italian navy, however, they were limited by the lack of spare parts, coal-firing, and the differences in armament between them and Italian vessels. Major modifications had to be carried out, and only two of them were used for any length of time before the Second World War, and even then only for secondary tasks.

Until the early 1920s the Italian navy did not even examine the possibility of building light cruisers, considering that its group of old 'esploratori' and pre-war cruisers was sufficient. This despite the fact that in 1922–23 France, her direct antagonist, had laid down three light cruisers of 7250 tons, armed with eight 155mm (6.1in) guns and twelve torpedo tubes (*Duguay-Trouin*, *Lamotte-Piquet*, *Primaguet*). However, when the French navy began building the twelve large destroyers of the *Jaguar* and *Lion* classes, displacing more than 2000 tons, armed with five 130mm guns and with a speed greater than 35kts, to supplement its first modest group of light cruisers, the Italian navy had to respond quickly in order to maintain the desired parity. The result was the four light cruisers of the *Di Giussano* type and twelve 'esploratori' of the *Navigatori* class. The balance, temporarily re-established by these measures, was disturbed anew in 1928 by the French when the *Jeanne d'Arc* and *Emile Bertin* were laid down, followed, in 1931–33, by the six 7600-ton units of the *La Galissonière* class. Italy responded first by starting construction of the second group of the 'Condottieri' programme (*Amando Diaz* and *Luigi Cadorna*), which represented an improvement on the preceding *Di Giussano* type. These were followed by the four units of the *Montecuccoli* and *Eugenio di Savoia* type, and the two *Garibaldi* units. At the beginning of the Second World War Italy, with her 12 light cruisers, had succeeded in counter-balancing the corresponding French units, disregarding the units included in subsequent design programmes or those just laid down.

GENERAL NOTES ON THE *DI GIUSSANO* CLASS CRUISERS

The four cruisers of the *Di Giussano* class were designed by the Navy Ministry's Committee of Naval Design under the direction of the Lieutenant General of the Naval Engineer Corps, Giuseppe Vian. Taking into account the specification of the French vessels, a displacement between 5000 and 6000 tons was considered adequate, and an armament of eight 152mm (6in) guns. Provided that protection was sacrificed, it would be possible to obtain high speed combined with sufficient range for operating in the Mediterranean. In order not to exaggerate initial hopes, these units were classified as '37-knot esploratori' in the design stage. The definitive classification of 'light cruiser' was assigned to them after they had entered service. The new cruisers were equal in every respect to the larger *Duguay-Trouin*, had a 4-knot greater maximum speed, and were superior to the large French destroyers in terms of armament and speed. The Italian navy estimated a requirement of six new units, but the usual financial difficulties forced a reduction in the number of units to four, with an option of building the other two (the *Diaz* class) in subsequent years.

The first three units, assigned the names of the famous 'Condottieri' (leaders of mercenary bands of military adventurers in Renaissance Italy) *Alberto di Giussano*, *Alberico da Barbiano* and *Bartolomeo Colleoni*, were contracted out to the Ansaldo yard in Genoa. The fourth, which was given the name of *Giovanni dalle Bande Nere*, was assigned to the Royal Yard of Castellammare di Stabia. The four cruisers were recorded in the Navy List by royal decree No 2354 on 1 December 1927.

The dates on which the four ships were laid down, launched and delivered were as follows:

Alberto di Giussano: laid down 29.3.1928, launched 27.4.1930, delivered 5.2.1931 = 35 months.
Alberico da Barbiano: laid down 16.4.1928, launched 23.8.1930, delivered 9.6.1931 = 36 months.
Bartolomeo Colleoni: laid down 21.6.1928, launched 21.12.1930, delivered 10.2.1932 = 44 months.
Giovanni dalle Bande Nere: laid down 31.10.1928, launched 27.4.1930, delivered 27.4.1931 = 30 months.

The cost of each unit, excluding armament and fire control equipment, was 59,170,000 lire.

TABLE 1: COMPARISONS WITH LIGHT CRUISERS OF FIRST WORLD WAR DESIGN

	Di Giussano	Enterprise	Omaha	Naka	Java	Emden
Laid down	1928	1918	1918	1922	1916	1921
In service	1931	1926	1923	1925	1925	1925
Standard displacement (tons)	5191	7580	7050	5195	6670	5600
Normal displacement	6571	8400	8400	5595	7050	6056
Full load displacement	6954	9350	9190	6850	—	6690
Dimensions (max) metres	169.3 × 15.5 × 5.1	174.0 × 16.6 × 5.9	169.5 × 16.8 × 6.1	162.8 × 14.2 × 5.0	155.3 × 16.0 × 5.5	155.1 × 14.3 × 5.93
feet	555.4 × 50.7 × 16.7	570.9 × 54.5 × 19.4	556.0 × 55.1 × 20.0	534.1 × 46.6 × 16.4	509.5 × 52.5 × 18.0	508.8 × 46.9 × 19.5
Geared turbines	2	4	4	4	3	2
Fuel	Oil	Oil	Oil	Oil	Oil	Oil
Power (shp)	95,000	80,000	90,000	90,000	72,000	46,000
Max normal speed (kts)	36.5–33	33	33.7	33–35	30.3	29
Range at 18kts (nm)	3800	4000	—	—	—	5300
Range at 15kts (nm)	—	—	10,000	—	3600	—
Range at 10kts (nm)	—	—	—	9000	—	—
Vertical armour (max, in mm)	24	76	76	63	75	50
Horizontal armour (max, in mm)	20	25	38	38	50	20
Main armament	8-152mm[1] (4 twin)	7-152mm[1] (1 twin, 6 single)	12-152mm[1] (2 twin, 8 single casemates)	7-140mm (7 single)	10-150mm (10 single)	8-150mm (8 single)
Secondary armament	6-100mm	5-102mm[2]	2-76mm[3]	2-80mm	4-75mm	2-88mm
Torpedoes	4 tubes	16 tubes	6 tubes	8 tubes	—	4 tubes
Aircraft	2	1	3	1	2	—
Catapults	1 forward	1 aft	2 midships	1 aft	2 midships	—
Mines	169	—	30	80	12	?

[1] 152mm = 6in; [2] 102mm = 4in; [3] 76mm = 3in

TABLE 2: COMPARISON WITH POST-1918 LIGHT CRUISER DESIGNS

	Di Giussano	Duguay-Trouin	Königsberg	Almirante Cervera
Laid down	1928	1922	1926	1922
In service	1931	1926	1929	1927
Standard displacement (tons)	5191	7249	6650	7475
Normal displacement	6571	7880	7400	7850
Full load displacement	6954	9350	8300	9327
Dimensions (max) metres	169.3 × 15.5 × 5.1	181.3 × 17.2 × 6.3	174.0 × 15.3 × 6.2	176.6 × 16.6 × 5.0
feet	555.4 × 50.7 × 16.7	594.8 × 56.4 × 20.7	570.9 × 50.2 × 20.3	579.4 × 54.5 × 16.4
Geared turbines	2	4	2 + 2 diesels	2
Fuel	Oil	Oil	Oil	Oil
Power (shp)	95,000	100,000	68,000	83,000
Max normal speed (kts)	36.5–37	33	32	34
Range at 18kts (nm)	3800	—	5750	—
Range at 15kts (nm)	—	4500	—	5000
Vertical armour (max, in mm)	24	20	50	76
Horizontal armour (max, in nm)	20	20	20	50
Main armament	8-152mm (4 twin)	8-155mm (4 twin)	9-155mm (3 triple)	8-152mm (3 twin, 2 single)
Secondary armament	6-100mm	4-75mm	2-88mm	4-102mm
Torpedoes	4 tubes	12 tubes	12 tubes	12 tubes
Aircraft	2	2	2	1*
Catapults	1 forward	1 aft	1 amidships	1 amidships*
Mines	169	—	—	—

* Added later

HULL AND SUPERSTRUCTURE

With an overall length of 169.3m (555ft 5in) and beam 15.5m (50ft 10in), the hull was constructed in steel using a hybrid system, in which the structural members were mainly longitudinal in the double bottom area, rising as far as the platforms, but transverse from the platforms to the main deck. Every third or every fourth transverse member was reinforced, where it was necessary to give support to a bulkhead. This design produced a structure which was fairly light in weight, but at the cost of overall strength; the ships' structural weakness was always considered one of their principal defects. The hull was reinforced by two longitudinal bulkheads which extended from the double bottom to the main deck, and from frame 9 forward to frame 173 aft. Transversely the hull was fitted with 15 watertight bulkheads which divided the hull into 16 compartments. All the passages between the hold and the third deck were sealed by watertight doors. The hull had a full-length main deck and a full-length second (battery) deck. The third deck was interrupted between frame 45 and frame 150 to allow space for the engine and boiler rooms. Below this there was a partial watertight platform. The height of the 'tween decks was 2.30m (7ft. 6in) between the main and second decks, and 2.15m (7ft) between the second and third decks.

The underwater hull was rather full-bodied, and there was considerable tumblehome above the waterline. The difference between maximum beam measured at the main deck and at the waterline was 1.80m (5ft 11in). This had been done with the aim of lightening the topsides whilst maintaining adequate underwater hull area, but the result was serious transverse instability. The weight of the tall superstructure, coupled with the defect just described, manifested itself in the ships' poor response to a beam or quarter sea, when they rolled very severely. In very rough seas the angle of roll reached 27–30 degrees, making shiphandling and life on board extremely difficult. The bilge keels, 80cm (2ft 8in) deep and 36m (118ft) long, only succeeded in relieving this unpleasant phenomenon to a slight extent. It is clear that gunnery was very badly affected by the instability of the hull.

The bow of the *Colleoni* and her sisters had a rather antiquated shape: straight with a slightly projecting ram underwater, to which was welded a bracket for the chains of the paravane anti-mine apparatus. The stern was of the rounded 'cruiser' type. The main deck was surmounted by a forecastle deck which extended from frame 132 to the extreme stem. The forecastle continued aft in the centre of the ship to form a deckhouse which contained the cowling of the forward funnel uptakes. Immediately abaft Turret 2 on the forecastle was the large superstructure whose lower section served as a hangar for the ship's two seaplanes. The aircraft entered the hangar via two broad sliding doors, one on each side of the hangar itself. The aircraft, on their trolleys, were transported on rails to the bow where the catapult was located.

Above the hangar were located the armoured conning tower, the anti-aircraft and anti-torpedo fire control stations, the radio room, the cipher office and other compartments. At a higher level, above the conning tower, there was the armoured fire control director with a 5-metre rangefinder. Abaft the other levels, in a narrower structure, were the small day cabin for the captain and the small space for the navigation officer and hydrophone office. At a yet higher level there were the charthouse and wheelhouse with two narrow bridge wings. At the top of the structure, 17.5m (57ft) above the waterline, there were two 90mm searchlights. The entire superstructure was straddled by a four-strut mast (tetrapod) whose legs extended down through the forecastle deck and the main deck to the second deck. At the top of this tetrapod, 26.5m (87ft) above the waterline, was the main fire control director.

TABLE 3: DATA RELATING TO TRANSVERSE STABILITY

	Ship loaded	Ship empty
Mean immersion	5.85m (19ft 2in)	4.39m (14ft 5in)
Corresponding displacement	7987.88 tons	5335.76 tons
Distance from centre of gravity to keel	5.75m (18ft 10in)	6.76m (22ft 2in)
Metacentric transverse radius	3.26m (10ft 8in)	4.58m (15ft 0in)
Effective metacentric radius	3.20m (10ft 6in)	4.50m (14ft 9in)
Height of centre of gravity above centre of underwater hull	2.30m (7ft 6in)	4.10m (13ft 6in)
Effective metacentric height	0.95m (3ft 1in)	0.47m (1ft 6in)
Moment of stability (Mx=Dr−a=tm)	7156.63 tons	2545.16 tons
Angle of zero stability	84 degrees	—
Angle of maximum righting moment	43.5 degrees	—

The large forward funnel, of elliptical cross-section and with an elegantly sinuous profile – the most obvious external characteristic of these vessels – trunked the exhaust of four boilers. A second deckhouse, located between frames 91 and 38, housed the uptakes of the two after boilers which discharged into a straight funnel of slightly oval section. The second deckhouse continued aft, housing secretaries' offices, cabins for the admiral, his chief of staff (when the ship was the divisional flagship), the commander and the officers' ward-room, and extended as far as the base of Turret 3.

Ten metres (33ft) aft of the after tunnel was a mast fitted with a derrick. Originally the lower section of this mast was a tripod, but when these ships' lack of stability became evident during initial sea trials, the tripod supports were removed, leaving only the vertical mast, itself considerably lower. The truck on the signal yard was 34.10m (112ft) above the waterline. Abaft the mast, above the wardroom, was located the after conning position surmounted in its turn by the after gun director (removed in 1933), also equipped with a 5-metre rangefinder. All the bridge splinter shields, which appear in the pictures of the ships when they were launched, were removed and replaced by guardrails, again with the aim of lightening the high parts of the ship.

Examination of the drawings will show clearly how the internal spaces of the ships were arranged, and a description is superfluous here. The three cruisers built by Ansaldo were virtually identical. The *Bande Nere*, built to the same design but by a different yard, did exhibit some slight differences compared with the others. As is also clear from the drawings, the cells of the double bottom below the engines and the spaces between the double bottom and the lower platforms were designed to hold fuel oil, while other cells held water for the boilers, drinking water, washing water and other lubricating oil.

PROTECTION

The protection of the *Di Giussano* class light cruisers was so 'light' that it can be considered non-existent. As a matter of standard policy, stretching back to very early times, the Italian navy has always given priority to speed over protection. Vast quantities of armour have been willingly sacrificed for the odd, and often illusory, knot more. The *Di Giussano* vessels were jokingly called 'cartoni animati' (animated cartoons) by their crews. The name was a pun: Walt Disney was then in fashion, but the reference was not to the merry goings-on of Micky Mouse, but to the strength of cardboard (Italian 'cartone').

The protection consisted of a belt of plates – between frame 28 at the bow and frame 173 at the stern – of special vanadium steel, 18mm thick at the extremities of the belt and 24mm towards the centre, where it covered the engine rooms and the midships magazine. A further band of plates, higher up, was also 20–24mm thick, while all the rest of the hull was built of standard plates, 12, 11, 10, 8 and 7mm thick. The side armour was sealed forward and aft by transverse members, 20mm thick. Inside the hull, about two metres from the side plates (the spacing varied because it was greater at the centre and less towards the extremities), ran two splinter-proof bulkheads, one to starboard and one to port, 20mm thick, again of vanadium steel. The entire chamber formed by the side plates and by the two transverse members, front and rear, was sealed above by a deck, corresponding to the second deck, formed of 20mm plates. These plates were of nickel-chrome steel on the *Colleoni*. At the bottom, between the side and the splinter-proof bulkhead, the space was sealed by a platform (corresponding to the second platform), consisting of 12mm plates.

The total weight of the vertical armour, on the *Colleoni*, was 290.8 tons and that of the horizontal armour 241 tons. The forward conning tower was constructed of 40mm plates, and the same thickness was used for the armoured trunk to the transmitting station. The fire control directors were protected by 25mm thick plates, and the main gun turrets by 22mm plates.

MACHINERY

The engines of the three cruisers built at Genoa were designed by Ansaldo. They comprised two groups of impulse turbines of the Belluzzo type, with single gearing, giving a total power of 100,000hp on the two shafts at full power. The total astern power was 40,000hp.

Each group consisted of one high pressure and one low pressure turbine, coupled at the shaft by means of reduction gears. Both turbines were equipped with astern rotors. The high pressure turbine consisted of a rotor with three compressor blade rings followed by a series of five multiple blade ring rotors for low cruising speeds and a second series of seven single blade ring rotors which came into action at high speed. On top of the three blade ring rotor a further three blade ring rotor was arranged which operated for astern running; this rotor also had three blade rings. Steam was routed through the turbine header for both directions of running.

The low pressure turbine was of the double efflux type and for each direction of flow it possessed ten single blade rings for normal cruising and three for astern running. Steam communication between high pressure and low pressure turbines was arranged between the two turbines and the exhaust from the low pressure ran directly to the condensors. With the two turbines developing 50,000hp per shaft (ie at maximum power), the high power turbine rotated at 2700rpm, while the low pressure turbine turned at 1800rpm. Each group of turbines was provided with one main condenser with a cooling area of 2030m² (21,850sq ft) and one auxiliary condenser with a cooling area of 90m² (969sq ft). The two groups of turbines were located in the hold below the second deck, in two separate watertight compartments (the starboard group between the watertight bulkheads located at frames 86 and 107 and the port group between the watertight bulkheads corresponding to frames 48 and 68), separated by a compartment containing two boilers. Each group, with its auxiliary machinery, was thus completely independent of the other. The forward engine installation powered the starboard screw and the after installation the port screw.

The two three-bladed screws were single castings, had a diameter of 4.40m (14ft 5in) a developed surface area of 12.52m² (135sq ft) and were designed for a maximum speed of 300rpm. The maximum permissible safe speed with a single screw rotating at 232/236rpm and the other disengaged (ie free to rotate)

was 26/28 kts, depending on the displacement. With one screw rotating at 150rpm and the other braked (ie with the screw locked), the maximum permissible speed was 14kts.

There were six boilers of the Yarrow-Ansaldo three-drum water-tube type with superheaters, arranged in three separate watertight compartments, two of them located forward of the starboard engine beyond the central magazine, and one between the port and starboard engine rooms. There were thus two boilers per room, positioned front to front. Each boiler had a power of 20,000hp with a heating surface of 6930m² (74,600sq ft) in the steam generating tubes and 1662m² (17,900sq ft) in the tubes of the six superheaters. Each boiler was served by 10 fuel sprayers; the steam temperature was 270 degrees. Feed water was supplied by means of four turbo supply pumps, and there were eight reciprocating pumps for auxiliary feed water. The feed water was pre-heated to 80–85 degrees.

On the second deck, above the forward engine room, there was a compartment for the two auxiliary boilers of the Yarrow type, which produced steam for the turbo dynamo, the auxiliary and cooling machinery, and for use in port. There were two groups of evaporators/condensors for the production of distilled water for the boilers. They were situated in the forward engine room and boiler rooms 5 and 6. The power plant control room was located on the second deck above the after engine room skylight.

The fuel oil reserves had a total capacity of 1290 tons, of which 1240 was useable; the remaining 50 tons were the non-combustible residue at the bottom. Each ship also carried 41 tons of lubricating oil for the turbines. Consumption of fuel oil was as follows:
Ship cruising at a constant speed of 18 kts, with average displacement of 7700 tons, all boilers functioning: approximately 11 tons per hour. Ship in port with normal on board services: approximately 17 tons per day.
The range of 18kts was calculated to be around 3800 miles; at 36kts it was 970 miles. The contract speed trials resulted in the following figures for each individual ship:

– *Colleoni* at 5565 tons, 312rpm = 39.85kts

– *Di Giussano* at 5812 tons, 304rpm = 38.50kts

– *Bande Nere* at 5550 tons, 307rpm = 41.11kts

– *Da Barbiano* at 5680 tons, 332rpm = 42.05kts

The figure for the *Da Barbiano* was obtained with the engines developing the extraordinary power of 123,479hp, and was maintained only for 32 minutes in the course of the test; the average speed was 39.6kts. All the speeds in the table were better than the contract speed which was 37kts.

Apart from the brilliant engines, these fantastic speeds could only be produced because of the excessively light hulls, as has already been noted. Normal speeds on duty were much lower, and when the ships came to take part in the Second World War, after a decade of service, their speed had dropped to 31–32kts.

ELECTRICAL PLANT

Electrical power was produced in two stations located on the platforms above the forward and aft engine rooms. Each station contained two 150kW turbo dynamos powered by 225hp turbines. The turbo dynamos produced direct current at 110 volts. In the forward drainage pump room there was a further turbo dynamo with a capacity of 52kW. A standard circuit distributed light and power around the vessel, while a double circuit, with two lines running along each side of the ship, supplied the motors powering the rudder, the turrets and the capstans. The main drainage pumps were also supplied by two independent circuits. The signal circuits, the radio room and the protected lighting were also provided with double electrical circuits.

The normal hourly consumption of energy was 100–120,000 watts, with consumption rising to 190,000 watts in combat. There were about 100 electric motors of varying power for running various pieces of machinery. An emergency 12-volt lighting system was fed by batteries having a capacity of 40 ampere-hours.

DAMAGE CONTROL

The central damage control station was in the space below the armoured deck between frames 160 and 164. For the purposes of ship's security the hull was subdivided into 11 zones, to each one of which was assigned a unit commanded by a non-commissioned officer. Zones 3 and 9 acted as secondary buoyancy control stations with their own crew and one officer.

Bilge pumps were installed as follows:

- 1 electric pump of 150 tons per hour forward of the forward magazine.

- 2 electric pumps of 50 tons per hour in the torpedo warhead store.

- 2 electric pumps of 60 tons per hour in the central magazine.

- 1 electric pump of 150 tons per hour abaft the after magazine.

Each of the forward and aft well rooms, the engine rooms and the boiler rooms contained a further two electric pumps of 50 tons per hour in each compartment, giving a total of 14 electric pumps.

It was possible to connect the starboard and port double bottoms below the five engine and boiler rooms, transferring liquids in either direction; this was intended to counter-balance the ship in case of flooding. If the ship was damaged in battle, the flooding and draining procedure could be too slow, but there was also an automatic balance system. This consisted of two pairs of longitudinal cofferdams which were always flooded with 360 tons of water when the ship was on active service. If any of the large central spaces were hit, the bulwark would rupture and the cofferdam on that side would automatically be connected to the sea. At the same time the cofferdam on the opposite side remained full. Normally the cofferdams were used to hold washing water and distilled water. The cofferdams 11, 12, 19 and 20 were filled with empty galvanized iron boxes.

The means of flooding were as follows: the forward and aft magazines were linked to the sea via Kingston floodgate valves of 350mm diameter. A further Kingston valve of 150mm diameter fed from the Kingston valve in the forward magazine could flood the torpedo warhead store. The midships magazine was connected to the sea by a Kingston valve of 250mm diameter. All the stores were also fitted with the usual pipework for a sprinkler system connected to the fire-fighting pipework. From the same pipework ran two pipes for flooding the small stores of oakum and petrol and further pipes for flooding the fuel oil stores.

STEERING GEAR

These ships had a single semi-balanced rudder, with a total surface area of 22.50m² (242sq ft) (16.20 for the blade, 6.30 for the balance portion). The maximum angle of deflection was 40 degrees. The steering gear consisted of four hydraulic oil-pressure cylinders arranged in pairs, whose pistons actuated the articulated connecting rods on the cross-piece of the steering gear. The cylinders were actuated by a variable capacity Williams-Jamey pump powered by a 100hp Brown Brothers electric motor.

In case of breakdown in the normal apparatus the rudder could be operated manually, using a pump of the same type as the electric one. The rudder could be controlled from four stations, one on the forward bridge, one in the conning tower, one in the armoured transmitting station and one on the after bridge. The commands were transmitted from the steering wheels to the servo motor via a hydraulic system using a fluid consisting of a mixture of water and glycerine.

COMPASSES

When the ships came into service they were equipped with one Sperry gyro compass situated in the transmitting station, with fourteen and later seventeen repeaters. The Sperry gyro compass was subsequently replaced by an Anschutz type with eighteen repeaters. By that time the ship was equipped with one magnetic compass in the upper bridge, two magnetic navigation compasses (one on the *Colleoni*) on the wings of the bridge, one manual device in the rudder room and two portable ones for use in the motor boats.

RADIO DIRECTION FINDING

The ships were fitted with a radio direction finding antenna which was located on the roof of the bridge.

BRIDGE EQUIPMENT

- Steering system: wheel with electro-hydraulic servo system.

- Transmission of orders: telephone equipment for communicating with Directors I and II, the engine control room, the manual steering system, the transmitting station and the armoured RT station. Pneumatic postal installation.

- Fire control: two target bearing transmitters linked with Directors I and II. Two telemetric data receivers connected to the directors, with enemy course and speed receiver.

- Night firing equipment (close to the conning tower): two fire control clocks, two 'Galileo' type gun direction sights, two order transmission tubes, one panel for switching the consoles to port and starboard. In the transmitting station there was a trunk for switching between normal and night firing.

COMMUNICATIONS

On board these ships there were four main radio transmitters – two on medium wave and two on short wave – and ten receivers. In addition to the radio direction finding equipment there was a submarine communications telegraph of the Spada type, situated in the hydrophone room, and an ultrasonic echo sounder. The broadcasting network was served by 10 loudspeakers. On the boat deck near the main mast there was a semaphore signalling station, linked by telephone to the bridge.

GROUND TACKLE

The ships were fitted with two 4-ton Hall anchors in hawseholes at the bow and one 2-ton anchor in a hawsehole at the stern. Each anchor was equipped with 11–12 lengths of chain (weight of each length 1420–1450kg, 3130–3195lb). To raise the anchors there were two cable holders (capstans) on the forecastle. The barrel of the capstan also served for the bow warps. The motors which operated the capstans were located underneath the main deck. Each capstan motor was independent of the other, but their transmissions were designed to allow one motor to operate both capstans in turn, should one motor fail. In case of total failure each capstan could be manually operated by means of capstan bars. The maximum power of each capstan was 8.5 tons for raising the anchor and 20 tons for lowering it. There were a further two capstans on the main deck aft for operating the stern anchor and the warps. These two capstans were also fitted with a system similar to that of the forward pair; they were powered by two separate but linkable electric motors located on the third deck.

CRANES AND DERRICKS
Each ship had two pairs of cranes for handling the boats positioned at either side of the forward funnel. A further two on either side were intended for operating the paravane equipment, while one collapsible 2.5-ton crane at the bow was used for recovering the seaplanes. A 10-ton derrick was fitted to the lower trunk of the after mast on the boat deck, for embarking supplies.

FOG AND SMOKE GENERATING EQUIPMENT
Four smoke machines were located in the boiler exhaust uptakes inside the forward funnel. They were operated from a platform forward of the funnel. Two artificial fog generators were fitted on either side at the stern; they were controlled from inside the ship. There was also a machine for producing coloured smoke located on the Director I platform.

HEALTH FACILITIES
On the main deck there was a seven-berth hospital, a further cabin which served as a first-aid post, an isolation ward with four beds and a decontamination chamber. During combat the first-aid post was used for treating the wounded, who were then berthed in other cabins. Extra space for first aid could be found in the petty officers' mess and the officers' library. The warrant officers' mess could be converted into a recovery room for men affected by mustard gas. The medical and para-medical staff consisted of two officers and six non-commissioned officers and ordinary seamen, assisted by seven stretcher bearers.

FOOD AND CLOTHING/REFRIGERATION/WASHING FACILITIES/HEATING
The victuals store was sufficient to supply the rations of 425 men for 60 days. The clothing store included 150 sets of uniforms, for distribution to crew members who were drafted directly on board in case of mobilisation. The ammunition cooling system comprised three water evaporation machines with a power of 21,000 refrigeration units per hour. A further machine (11,000 refrigeration units per hour) cooled the meat and vegetable stores. One machine was kept for the production of ice. On the starboard side of the main deck there was a steam laundry for the crew's clothing. The crew's quarters were heated by means of steam heaters. There was also an air conditioning plant for the admiral's quarters and the briefing room.

BOATS
In peacetime the following boats were carried (in wartime many of them were disembarked):
Rowing and sailing boats:
– two 8.60m (28ft) launches (2.36m, 7¾ft beam – 8 oars).

TABLE 4: CHARACTERISTICS OF THE 152mm GUNS

Year of construction	1927–1929
Weight of gun excluding breech mechanism	7340kg (7.22 tons)
Weight of breech mechanism	355kg (0.35 tons)
Weight of cradle (for two guns)	6600kg (6.5 tons)
Weight of mount (for two guns)	13,100kg (12.9 tons)
Weight of installation excluding armour	71,900kg (70.8 tons)
Total weight of installation including armour	85,000kg (83.7 tons)
Angle of elevation	45 degrees
Angle of depression	5 degrees
Muzzle velocity of projectile	900ms, 2950fps (shot), 935ms, 3070fps (shell)
Weight of projectile	47.5kg, 105lbs (shot)
Weight of charge	15.5kg, 34lbs (shot)
Maximum range	26,000m, 28,500yds (shot) 25,200m, 27,500yds (shell)
Heel of ship during fire	10 degrees

N.B. In the above 'shot' corresponds to AP (or armour-piercing) shell, and 'shell' to high explosive (or HE)

– one/two 4.50m (14¾ft) boats (1.64m, 5 1/3ft, beam – 4 oars).
– one 3.83m (12½ft) dinghy (1.37m, 4½ft, beam – 2 oars).
– two 8.50m (27¾ft) gigs (1.00m, 3¼ft, beam – 12 oars).
– one 'Snipe' recreational sailing dinghy (4.72 × 1.52m, 15½ft × 5ft).
motor boats:
– one 10m (32¾ft) admiral's barge (50–60hp).
– one 20m (65½ft) motor pinnace.
– one 6m (19¾ft) seppietta motor boat (20–25hp).
– one 10m diesel launch (40–45hp).
– one 10m fast motor boat (25hp).

In 1936 the 8.50m gigs were replaced by two motor launches of the same size.

ARMAMENT
The main armament of the *Colleoni* and the other light cruisers of her class, in accordance with the standard adopted by all major navies, was the 152mm (6in) gun. The eight 152mm/53cal guns, built by Ansaldo at Terni, were arranged in four twin centreline mountings, two forward and two aft, in turrets of rectangular plan-form. The turrets were constructed of 22mm steel plate, with a total weight, excluding guns, of 11 tons. The turrets had a field of fire of about 300 degrees.

The normal supply of 152mm rounds stored in the two magazines (forward and aft) was 280 rounds in all, of which 140 were 'shot' and 140 shells. In wartime it was possible to increase these figures by about 50 per cent. The claimed rate of firing for the 152mm Ansaldo guns was 6 rounds per minute, but in reality it was 4 rounds. The guns built by Ansaldo had a slower loading system than those built subsequently by Odero-Terni-Orlando, which were faster but less robust. In the Ansaldo model the gun was loaded at a fixed elevation (around 20 degrees). The loader which transferred the shell to the breech remained in position while the rammer pushed it into the gun (a period of 5–6 seconds). In the succeeding OTO models a reciprocating lever transferred the shell onto the loader, and while the rammer pushed it into the gun – at any elevation – the lever descended to collect a further shell, ready to transfer it onto the loader the moment the preceding round had been fired. Thus the loading cycle was reduced from 14 seconds for the Ansaldo guns to 7 seconds for the OTO gun, firing at high speed and with a competent crew.

All the 152mm gun types used by the Italian navy employed the same type of ammunition, and all suffered from excessive longitudinal dispersion in firing. The extent of this defect was unpredictable and highly variable, which made it all the more difficult for the gun director to estimate the degree of inaccuracy at a distance, and hence by how much to compensate. The problem was a result of various factors, the most important of which was the imprecise construction of the shells and charges which nearly always varied in weight. The guns also had their faults: they were complex and excessively light. Various modifications were carried out aimed at reducing the dispersion, and one of the changes was to reduce the muzzle velocity of the shell by about 100ms. However, the dispersion remained very high, in spite of all the measures taken. In later models of 152mm gun built by Ansaldo in 1934, and by OTO in 1936, the barrel length was increased to 55 calibres in an attempt to obtain improved thermodynamic performance, and these new guns were in fact more accurate.

Another problem common to nearly all types of Italian gun was the high percentage of rounds which simply did not fire, because of mechanical faults or delays in loading. The proportion of failed rounds was anything up to 10 per cent, and could be blamed on both the ammunition and the guns themselves. The breech closure, the loaders, the hoists and the action of the primer were all liable to give problems. When a fault occurred, the gun had to cease firing until the problem was solved, or, if the shell could not be fired, the gun could not be used again in that action.

Some years later, Admiral Iachino, who for a long period was Commander of the Italian Fleet in wartime, wrote the following: 'This state of affairs was a source of very grave anxiety to us, since the practical result was that our ships' armament was severely reduced, which could place us in a position of effective inferiority to the enemy, even when this inferiority, in theory at least, did not exist . . . The matter was made even more serious by the fact that we were confronted by a navy like the British, whose artillery was decidedly more efficient than ours, both in terms of the smaller proportion of failed rounds, and for the extent of dispersion, which, as we all know, was much better than ours.'

The secondary armament consisted of six 100mm/47cal (3.9in) RM OTO model 1928 guns in twin mountings behind 8mm shields, located two on deck sided amidships and the third on a centreline elevated platform forward of the second funnel.

The number of rounds stored in the midships magazine was 2400 shells and 240 starshells. In wartime it was possible to increase these figures by 50 per cent. The above 100mm/47 OTO dual purpose installations were the normal secondary armament for Italian heavy and light cruisers. The gun was a copy of the Austrian Skoda 1910, but fitted with an interchangeable loose liner. It was a gun of good ballistic qualities and accuracy, but by then of antiquated design. The mounts, designed by Commander Minisini, allowed manual loading at any elevation, in that the cradle trunnions were raised automatically as the gun elevated to give the necessary breech clearance. Although ingenious, the system proved to be unable to make the rapid changes of elevation necessary when following fire control directions against increasingly fast-flying aircraft and against new forms of low level attack. In practice Italian cruisers, and in particular those which are at present under discussion, began the Second World War with an anti-aircraft gun which was heavy and of only modest efficiency, suitable for barrage defence but little else.

Until the Summer of 1940 the anti-aircraft armament of these cruisers consisted of two 40mm/39 (2pdr) guns in single installations (located at the level of the armoured conning tower abreast the rear legs of the tetrapod), and

TABLE 5: CHARACTERISTICS OF THE 100mm/47 GUNS

Weight of gun excluding breech mechanism	1848kg (1.8 tons)
Weight of breech mechanism	83kg (183lbs)
Weight of cradle (for two guns)	847kg (1867lbs)
Weight of mount (for two guns)	8352kg (8.2 tons)
Total weight of mounting excluding shield	12,922kg (12.7 tons)
Total weight of shielded installation	14,542kg (14.3 tons)
Angle of elevation	45 degrees
Muzzle velocity or projectiles	880ms (2890fps)
Maximum range	15,240m (16,650yds)

TABLE 6: CHARACTERISTICS OF THE 40mm/39 VICKERS-TERNI MOD 1915 AUTOMATIC GUNS

Weight of gun	347kg (765lbs)
Weight of mount	505kg (1133lbs)
Muzzle velocity of shell	600ms (1970fps)
Effective range	4500m (4900yds)
	(theoretically 7000m or 7650yds)
Theoretical rate of firing	200 rounds per minute
	(effectively 50 because of frequent jamming)
Amunition carried	2000 rounds per gun
Crew	one aimer and four gun crew

eight 13.2mm guns in twin installations, located two on the hangar roof, immediately abaft the conning tower, and two on the roof of the after conning position. Bases for a further two mountings were fitted on the roof of the upper bridge. Subsequently the 40mm/39 guns were replaced by four more efficient twin 20mm/65 mountings located two on the conning tower deck in place of the 40mm guns, and two on the after deckhouse abaft the funnel.

The 20mm/65 machine gun, developed in the period 1930–1935, in single or twin installations, was the most widely employed anti-aircraft gun on Italian ships during the Second World War. The gun was operated by one aimer and four gun crew.

The Breda 13.2mm gun, the smallest of the 'heavy automatic guns' used in the Italian navy (below this calibre the light arms were designated 'machine guns'), was derived from the French Hotchkiss machine gun of the same calibre. The design requirements of the gun were defined in 1931. It was installed widely on all types of vessel in single or twin installations. It was of good quality, but offered insufficient power against the aircraft brought into service in the course of the Second World War, in particular because the shell was not explosive, which limited the amount of damage it could inflict.

FIRE CONTROL AND TRANSMISSION OF ORDERS

Normal director firing (all guns on one target)
Direction – from Director I (in fore top) and Director II (above the armoured conning tower).
Fire control – The transmitting station (main control centre) was linked to the General Fire Control apparatus (APG) of Directors I and II. The two directors had their own rangefinders and a further two rangefinders were also situated in

TABLE 7: CHARACTERISTICS OF THE 20mm/65 BREDA AUTOMATIC GUN

Weight of gun	68.5kg (151lbs)
Total weight of twin mounting	2330kg (2.1 tons)
Effective range	5500m (6000yds)
Theoretical rate of firing	250 rounds per minute
Ammunition carried	19,200 rounds per mounting

TABLE 8: CHARACTERISTICS OF THE 13.2mm MACHINE GUN

Weight of single gun	47.5kg (105lbs)
Weight of mount	600kg (1323lbs)
Weight of complete twin mounting	695kg (1532lbs)
Maximum range	6000m (6500yds)
Rate of fire	400 rounds per minute
Ammunition carried	2400 rounds per gun
Crew	one aimer and three gun crew

Turrets 2 and 3, which also had auxiliary fire control stations. In the event of damage, it was possible to bypass Turret 2's, but not Turret 3's, control station by using the APG of Director II.

Laying and aiming – could be linked to the APG or direct.

Divided fire control

Direction – Forward artillery group (Turrets 1 and 2) from Director II and the after artillery group (Turrets 3 and 4) from Director I.

Fire control – Forward group from the fire control station of Turret 2; after group from the transmitting station.

Laying and aiming – linked to the relevant APG or direct.

Independent firing (not using the APG equipment of the directors)

Direction – From Turrets 2 and 3 equipped with periscopes for observing fire.

Fire control – Fire control station of Turrets 2 and 3.

Laying and aiming – Direct for the superfiring turrets, linked to the superfiring turrets for the lower turrets, or direct for all turrets.

Anti-aircraft fire

Firing was controlled by the gun captains based on the target distance transmitted to them by means of loudspeakers or telephone from the anti-aircraft director station and based on their own estimation.

EARLY WARNING SYSTEM

Look-outs equipped with binoculars; located as follows:

– 2 look-outs per side on the platform adjacent to Director I.

– 3 look-outs per side on the conning tower deck.

– 5 look-outs per side on the Admiral's bridge.

– 2 look-outs per side near the after director (until it was removed).

AMMUNITION

152mm ammunition: Each magazine was provided with a cage-type hoist for embarking and disembarking ammunition. The cage could contain 8 propellant charges or 12 shells. The ammunition was transferred from the supply lighter via loading doors located in the hull sides close to the hoists.

100mm ammunition: The dredger hoists between the magazine and the guns were reversible, and could thus be used for embarking ammunition. Loading was a manual operation.

Supply to the guns: Each 152mm turret was fed by two electric dredger hoists. There were also two cage elevators which acted as an auxiliary supply method. The hoists revolved with the turrets and ran directly to the magazine. The 100mm installations were supplied by hoists which carried the ammunition from the midships magazine directly to the deck. From that point supplies were transferred by hand. Mounting No 3, situated high up and hence difficult to supply, was equipped with small ready-use reserves of ammunition.

The machine guns were supplied from the entry lobby of the midships magazines. Appropriate small reserves were kept next to each gun for immediate use.

SMALL ARMS

On board each ship there were 235 6.5mm mod 91 carbines; three 8mm machine guns; fifty 7.65mm Berretta automatic pistols; 2 Berretta machine rifles.

RANGEFINDERS

– Two 5.00m (16.4ft) coincidence type in 152mm Turrets 2 and 3.

– Two 5.00m stereoscopic type in the main directors.

– Two 3.00m (9.8ft) rangefinders in the secondary directors for surface fire with the 100mm guns.

– One 3.00m on the after director (later removed) for torpedo fire, with two small gun direction sights on the Admiral's bridge.

On the conning tower level there were two sights and two fire control clocks for the direction of the main armament at night.

TORPEDOES

The torpedoes carried on these cruisers were the SI (Silurificio Italiano) 250/533 (533mm, or 21in, calibre), which weighed 1.7 tons and were capable of 41 kts over a distance of 4000m (4300yds), 31kts over a distance of 8000m (8750yds) and 26kts over a distance of 12,000m (13,000yds). Four torpedoes were stowed in the launching tubes and two were stored in containers alongside the after deckhouse. The torpedo tubes were two twin San Giorgio installations, located on the main deck, abreast the after funnel. It took about 30 minutes to reload a torpedo tube after firing.

DEPTH CHARGES

Each cruiser initially carried sixteen 100kg (220lb) depth charges which could be dropped, with a further twenty-four of the 50kg (110lb) type in reserve. On the after deck, abreast the propeller guards, there were two Menon type depth charge throwers, and a discharge rail for depth charges could also be fitted.

MINESWEEPING EQUIPMENT

The ships were fitted with three self-protective anti-mine paravanes, with a depth of sweep of 9m (30ft), and capable of sweeping a zone 100m (330ft) wide.

MINES

The cruisers of the *Di Giussano* class, in common with virtually all Italian light cruisers, were equipped for minelaying. The equipment consisted of iron rails (one day's work to set them up on deck), which ran from the sides of the after deckhouse to the extreme stern; the run could be made shorter, depending on the quantity of mines to be embarked.

It was possible to embark up to 169 'Bollo' type mines or 157 'Elia' type mines for an overall weight of about 111 tons, although this meant that the after turrets could not be worked and the torpedo tubes could no longer be trained. 92 'Bollo' type mines or 78 'Elia' type could be embarked without obstructing the guns.

AIRCRAFT

The catapult for launching the ship's aircraft was on the centreline of the forecastle, pointing over the bow. The first catapult fitted, of the explosive-propelled 'Magaldi' type, was replaced by a compressed air 'Cagnotto' type which provided a maximum cradle speed of 35ms (115fps) on the 24m (79ft) long catapult track. The cradle consisted of a fabricated steel structure with four wheels. The aircraft was retained with hooks which disengaged automatically when the end of the track was reached. Prior to launching, the aircraft and cradle were held stationary by a small copper bar which disintegrated under a tractive force of 3000kg (6600lb), at which point the carriage was released to start its run.

Initially these ships carried two seaplanes of the CRDA Cant 25 AR type, a version of the Cant 25 with folding wings. This was a single-engined flying boat of metal, wood and canvas construction, fitted with stabilising floats under the wings. The pusher propeller was powered by a 410hp Fiat engine, giving the aircraft a maximum speed of 425km/hr (265mph). Wingspan was 8.45m (27ft 9in) fuselage length 10.40m (34ft 2in). All-up weight was 1700kg (3750lbs). In 1938 these aircraft were replaced by the IMAM Ro 43 spotter floatplane, a good reconnaissance aircraft but one whose flight performance and armamant were very rapidly surpassed in the early years of the war. Its characteristics are given in table 9.

The aircraft were stowed in the hangar under the bridge. Two pairs of rails ran from the hangar, one along each side of the forecastle, abreast the forward turrets, and joined up at points where they met the catapult tracks. A collapsible derrick boom capable of lifting up to 2.5 tons could be set up on the forecastle to hoist the aircraft back on board. Launching orders were given from the bridge by telephone or by displaying disc signals: white (prepare for take-off), green (take off) and red (abort take-off). The bow position of the catapult gave rise to numerous problems. Prior to the aircraft taking off, the ship had to be manoeuvred directly into wind, and even when the sea was only slightly rough the vessel's pitching movements and the effects of sea spray made the launch very difficult if not downright impossible.

PROJECTED DESIGNS FOR CONVERTING THE *DI GIUSSANO* CLASS INTO ANTI-AIRCRAFT CRUISERS

In the years immediately preceding the Second World War, the General Staffs of the world's major navies began to be concerned at the possible danger to warships from aircraft. Although the small-scale conflicts in this period had offered little scope for judging the issue, it was clear that aircraft now represented a real threat, since they had become vastly more efficient and menacing compared with the primitive machines which had operated during the First World War. In fact, some theoretical studies considered that aircraft would soon be the determining factor in any conflict at sea.

TABLE 9: CHARACTERISTICS OF THE IMAM Ro 43 AIRCRAFT

Wingspan	9.71m (31ft 10in)
Height	3.51m (11ft 6in)
Wing area	33.36m² (359sq ft)
Engine	9-cylinder Piaggio PXR radial, developing 700hp
Maximum speed	300km/hr at 2000m (186mph at 6500ft)
Ceiling	6500m (21,000ft)
Range	1500km (930 miles)
Armament	two 7.7mm machine guns
All-up weight	1760kg (3880lb); fully loaded 2400kg (5290lb)

In spite of the increase in the number of anti-aircraft guns carried on the larger ships, and the protection offered by the aircraft embarked on the aircraft carriers now possessed by some navies, there was a clear need to increase shipborne defences; it was widely thought essential to produce a specialized type of ship for advanced anti-aircraft defence of naval formations, and in particular the defence of the aircraft carriers, which were bound to be the principal targets of the enemy air force.

In Britain an effective solution was found in the conversion into anti-aircraft units of the small 'C' light cruisers, built at the end of the First World War. The first two were withdrawn from service and converted in 1935–36, and others were modified later; the five or six 6in guns were removed and replaced by eight or ten 4in guns, and numerous 40mm, 2pd and 20mm machine guns.

In Italy the problem was not treated seriously enough. Projected conversions foundered on the fundamental difficulty that Italy lacked a really efficient anti-aircraft gun at that time. In the mid-1930s Ansaldo had carried out design studies for a 90mm (3.5in) anti-aircraft gun, initially 48 calibres and later 50 calibres long. The new gun was required in order to provide an anti-aircraft weapon of real effectiveness for the new 35,000-ton *Littorio* type battleships and the two *Doria* class battleships which were undergoing major modernisation. The new gun was mounted in a cradle which allowed up to 75 degrees of elevation. The pedestal of the installation was stabilized in the roll plane, while the central support pivot was stabilized in the pitch plane. The stabilization system was based on an automatic gyroscope which controlled two electric motors operating simultaneously on worm screws. Each single installation was protected by a completely enclosed 'turret' of oval form. The shield was thicker at the front, to help balance the mass of the gun as well as to increase protection. The turret was enclosed at the bottom with a baseplate. The turret and baseplate were both connected to the mount's central pivot, and were therefore part of the stabilized mass which could be trained. In other words, the entire turret was supported on the pivot, which, in theory, remained horizontal, regardless of the ship's rolling and pitching. In practice the efficiency of the stabilizing mechanisms was often compromised by their delicacy and by frequent breakdowns in the electrical installation. The maximum range of the 90mm gun was more than 10,000m (11,000yds) and the rate of firing – the gun was loaded manually – was 12–15 rounds per minute.

In 1936–37, when it became evident that this new anti-aircraft weapon might come into service in the very near future, studies were begun into the feasibility of converting the *Di Giussano* class into anti-aircraft cruisers, as they were no longer considered to be first rate ships. The first design, completed in February 1938, provided for the removal of all the existing artillery and the installation of sixteen single 90mm/48 turrets, arranged six forward, four midships and six aft, supplemented by ten twin 20mm machine gun mountings arranged on the deckhouse to either side of the after funnel. The fire control equipment was to be fitted on the slightly modified bridgework, from which the hangar was to be removed. Further conversion work would have included modifying the forward and aft magazines to handle 90mm ammunition, and altering the midships magazine for ammunition for the 90mm guns and the 20mm machine guns. Each magazine would have been linked to the single high-angle 90mm mountings by means of hoists protected by 20mm steel plates. The areas of deck on which the 90mm installations would be mounted were to be reinforced by 30mm thick nickel-chrome steel plates. This extra armour added to the existing 20mm plate of the second deck and the 24mm and 28mm thick longitudinal bulkheads, would have improved markedly the ship's horizontal protection. The removal of the 152mm turrets would have saved the same amount of weight as that added by the new armament (each 90mm 'turret' weighed about 20 tons) and the added protection.

At the same time the OTO (Odero-Terni-Orlando) yard had also been commissioned by the Navy Ministry to draw up detailed conversion plans for these ships, and the design was presented in March 1938. This time the planned modifications were more radical, although the arrangement of the 90mm guns was identical to the earlier design. The forward superstructure was to be completely redesigned, and would have been lower and wider than the existing one. The tetrapod mast would have been removed altogether, and four fire control directors were to be set up on the new structure. This arrangement would have provided independent control for the three groups of 90mm guns and twenty 20mm machine guns arranged in two groups of five twin installations, each group mounted on two large stabilised platforms, located forward of the after funnel, one to starboard and one to port. The concentration of 20mm machine guns would have provided a means of directing a considerable volume of fire on individual targets.

A further design was presented by the Naval Design Committee in June 1938. This plan differed from its predecessors in the substitution of four of the aft 90mm guns by two twin 135mm/45 (5.3in) OTO installations. This was a new anti-ship weapon, designed to arm the light cruisers of the *Capitani Romani* class (in triple mountings the 135mm was also intended to constitute the secondary anti-ship armament for the *Doria* class battleships). The 135mm/45 guns, which were amongst the best arms manufactured in Italy in the period between the two World Wars, fired a 32kg (70lb) shell a distance of 19,600m (21,500yds) at a rate of six rounds per minute. This last plan therefore foresaw the replacement of half of the vessels' anti-ship armament by more modern guns, which were more efficient than the old 152mm guns in so far as dispersion was much reduced. The new armament would have necessitated a variation in the conversion of the after magazine and the installation of a different system for fire control, consisting of a director with a 6m (20ft) base rangefinder, linked to an electro-mechanical fire control centre. The number of directors for the 90mm guns would have been reduced to three, capable of controlling fire against three separate targets.

Regardless of the design selected – one of the two entirely anti-aircraft plans or the compromise anti-aircraft version with an admittedly limited anti-ship component – the Italian navy would have had at its disposal a number of vessels capable of providing very effective anti-aircraft defence to a fleet or convoy. As all of the plans discussed here left the power plants unchanged, these ships, which were still fast, would have been capable of escorting formations of high-speed ships, giving them effective defence against attack from the air. The fact that none of these plans came to fruition was due to financial problems on the one hand, and on the other to the navy's reluctance to adopt so radical a solution to a problem which in 1938 was still theoretical. It is likely that the

anti-aircraft armament of the larger vessels, added to that of the escort ships, was thought to be sufficient to keep the slow aircraft of the time at bay. The decision not to proceed was also influenced by the slow rate of production of the new guns, and the urgent need for them on battleships. It was certainly a mistake to have underestimated the advantage of producing anti-aircraft ships quickly, even if they were of a makeshift nature. Instead the problem was shelved in favour of working on new vessels; these were the two ex-Thai cruisers *Taksin* and *Naresuan*, which were under construction at the Adriatic and Trieste yards. Requisitioned at the start of the war, they were renamed *Etna* and *Vesuvio*, but their construction proceeded so slowly that, when the Armistice was signed at the end of 1943, they were only 60 per cent complete.

SERVICE CAREER

The light cruiser *Bartolomeo Colleoni*, built at the Ansaldo yard at Genoa, was launched on 21 December 1930. Completed and delivered to the Royal Italian Navy on 10 February 1932, she was assigned to II Naval Squadron (comprising exclusively light fast ships), based at La Spezia.

In the course of the Spanish Civil War Italy gave substantial assistance to the Nationalist forces, without taking an active part in the conflict. The *Colleoni* carried out a mission to Barcelona between 5 September and 3 October 1936 for the protection of the Italians resident there; she completed four missions escorting merchant ships loaded with troops and supplies (January–May 1937); and in January–February 1937 the ship carried out three patrol missions aimed at intercepting traffic directed towards the Republican ports, and signalling its presence to the Nationalist authorities.

While the protracted Sino-Japanese conflict persisted, Italy, in common with many other European nations, maintained a naval force in the Far East to guard national interests and the rights of resident Italians. In November 1938 the *Colleoni* was sent to replace the cruiser *Raimondo Montecuccoli*, which was returning home after a long sojourn in Eastern waters. The *Colleoni* arrived at Shanghai, which had been occupied by the Japanese a year earlier, on 23 December 1938, and remained on station until October 1939. The war in Europe had started by that time, and Japan, profiting from their involvement in the conflict, had requested that the European powers withdraw their ships.

When Italy entered the war (10 June 1940) the *Colleoni* was a member of II Division of II Squadron, together with the *Bande Nere*, which was the flagship of the division. The two ships were transferred to Palermo. On the evening of the day that Italy declared war the *Bande Nere* and the *Colleoni* sailed from Palermo in order to mine the Sicilian Channel. From 22 to 24 June the division left port again to carry out a fruitless search for French ships reported West of Sardinia. At the end of June, after the signing of the armistice with France, the division left Palermo and transferred to Augusta, on the Eastern coast of Sicily. A further unsuccessful search mission was carried out during 2 and 3 July and on the 4th the two cruisers escorted a convoy steaming from Tripoli.

TABLE 10: **FATES OF THE *DI GIUSSANO* CLASS CRUISERS**

Bartolomeo Colleoni	Sunk in battle, 19 July 1940, by the cruiser *Sidney* off Cape Spada (Crete)
Alberto di Giussano	Torpedoed and sunk, 13 December 1941, by the British
Alberico da Barbiano	destroyers *Sikh*, *Maori*, *Legion* and the Dutch destroyer *Isaac Sweers* of Cape Bon (Tunisia)
Giovanni dalle Bande Nere	Torpedoed and sunk, 1 April 1942, 8 miles off Stromboli (Lipari Islands) by HM Submarine *Urge*

Between 7 and 10 July the two units of II Division went out to escort a large convoy heading for Bengazi, together with other ships. Considerable Italian forces went to sea to provide long-distance protection of the convoy, in response to similar movements on the part of the British fleet. The result was the battle of Punta Stilo, in which II Division did not take part, as its task was to ensure that the convoy arrived undamaged at Cirenaica. From Bengazi II Division was transferred to Tripoli in order to keep the ships clear of English aircraft operating from their Egyptian bases.

THE BATTLE OF CAPE SPADA, 19 JULY 1940, AND THE SINKING OF THE *BARTOLOMEO COLLEONI*

The presence of II Division at Tripoli gave the High Command of the Italian Navy the idea of sending the two ships out to bombard the British coastal positions at Sollum, after which they were to make for the base of Portolago, at Lero in the Dodecanese, from which point they were intended to disrupt British shippping in the Aegean by carrying out swift strikes. The bombardment of Sollum was subsequently cancelled from the programme because it was not considered useful by the High Command in Libya; the two ships thus left Tripoli on the evening of 17 July, heading towards the Aegean, passing North of Crete. They were intended to reach Portolago at 1400 on the 19th.

On the same day (19 July) the Commander of the British Mediterranean Fleet had ordered four destroyers of the Second Flotilla (*Hyperion*, *Ilex*, *Hero* and *Hasty*) to carry out an anti-submarine hunt in the channel between Caso and Crete. The Australian cruiser *Sidney* and the destroyer *Havock* were ordered to search the Gulf of Athens to prepare the way for a convoy due to leave Egypt in the near future. At the same time a further eight destroyers were stationed in the Southern Aegean to assist in the passage of another convoy, also sailing from Egypt, and to receive yet another coming from the Dardanelles. It was therefore inevitable that the two Italian cruisers, which were to carry out the planned disruptive action, would encounter considerable enemy opposition, and were unlikely to be successful in their mission.

Around 0600 on 19 July the two Italian cruisers entered the channel between Crete and Cerigotto, zigzagging at 25kts. The sea was very rough, with a strong mistral wind blowing, and the sun was rising precisely over the bow. At that point the four English destroyers of the Second Flotilla, spaced 1000m (1000yds appoximately) apart, came into view. At the moment of sighting, the two formations were about 17,000m (18,500yds) apart. At the same time the *Sidney* and the *Havock* were about 60 miles distant, steaming North towards the Gulf of Athens.

Immediately after the sighting the four English destroyers signalled their discovery and steamed away to the North-East; the *Sidney*, having received the signal, altered course towards South, making for the destroyers. The *Bande Nere* was carrying the Italian Admiral Ferdinando Casardi, flag officer of II Division; he saw that the destroyers were withdrawing and thought that they might be the advance escort of a convoy, so he set off in pursuit, increasing speed to 32kts and opening fire (0627) with the 152mm guns at the two nearest ships, which were 17,000m (18,500yds) distant at that point. At that range it was inevitable that the British salvoes in reply fell short, and for the same reason, the several torpedoes launched (0643) did not hit the target. The firing lasted until 0650, when the destroyers used their superior speed to take them out of firing range, covering themselves by making smoke. The Italian cruisers at once changed course to starboard in order to shorten the range, but when the British ships reappeared they were 23,000m (25,000yds) distant, and the last salvoes fired by the Italians had no effect. The two formations continued to steam on slightly convergent courses, with the British ahead and completely out of range.

The Italian admiral had no information at all on the general situation in the area. Because of the state of the sea, and in order not to waste time, he had decided against launching his reconnaissance aircraft (they were rarely used by the Italians in any case). Nor did he have the promised support from the reconnaissance aircraft stationed in the Italian airfields around the Aegean; they had been set to fly their missions in the early hours of the morning, but had not been able to take off for various technical reasons (they did get airborne later and arrived at the scene after the encounter had taken place).

It was thus a complete surprise for the units of II Division when, around 0730, salvoes of medium calibre shells fell close to them, fired from port through a bank of low, dense fog. Of the new adversary, all they could see through the fog were the flames from the guns. The shells came from HMAS *Sidney*, 12,000m (13,000yds) away from the Italian cruisers, steaming towards the South-East on a convergent route. The fire, directed at the *Bande Nere*, was accurately aimed, and immediately a 6in (152mm) shell hit the vessel close to the after funnel.

The *Bande Nere* and the *Colleoni* immediately started firing but, with nothing but the flames sporadically appearing in the gloom to aim at, they were unable to find the correct range. The cruisers immediately turned 90 degrees to starboard, continuing to fire with the after turrets. Their salvoes were not accurate, and only one lucky shell hit the *Sidney* on the after funnel, without causing serious damage. However, the shells from their unseen enemy were falling very close to the Italian ships, and they were forced to emit a smoke screen. When the screen cleared, the Italian ships turned South with the *Sidney* 19,000m (21,000yds) astern, followed by the *Havock*. Meanwhile the four destroyers of the Second Flotilla had reversed direction, and were rejoining the formation. At 0753 the Italian units were making for Cape Spada, still followed by the *Sidney*, which resumed fire on the *Colleoni* once the ship was within range. The pursuing destroyers were still out of range.

At this point the situation was still reasonably favourable to the Italians, who had at their disposal sixteen 152mm calibre guns compared with the eight of the *Sidney*, and had nothing to fear from the twenty 4.7in (120mm) guns of the destroyers, as they could keep out of their range. They also had a slight margin of speed over the *Sidney*; in theory the Australian ship was capable of 32.5kts but in fact her maximum speed was no better than 30–31kts, whereas the Italian cruisers, although their brilliant performance of yore was now much reduced, could still exceed 32kts. It has always been true, however, that the ship which tries to shorten the distance, rather than fight at the limit of his guns' range, gains the advantage. The heavy seas put the Italian cruisers at a disadvantage, as it made them roll severely (a serious defect of the *Di Giussano* class), making fire control difficult; as they were firing at long range, the chances of hitting the enemy target were even slighter. For this reason it was likely that the encounter would come to a conclusion either when the distance between the two contenders became too great for combat, or when a fortunate shell struck and weakened one of the two adversary units, and that was just what happened.

At 0824, when the Italian cruisers had steamed five miles beyond Cape Spada and had almost rounded Cape Kimaros, the *Colleoni* was struck by an accurate salvo from the *Sidney*. The rudder was put out of action, but jammed in the central position, so the ship remained on course. Immediately afterwards the Italian cruiser was hit again, in the midships area and the armoured

TABLE 11: **PARTICULARS OF THE *ALBERTO DI GIUSSANO* CLASS LIGHT CRUISERS**

HULL DETAILS

Dimensions and weights

Overall length	169.32m (555ft 6in)
Length between perpendiculars	160.00m (524ft 11in)
Waterline length	167.20m (548ft 6in)
Max beam outside plating	15.59m (51ft 2in)
Depth	9.90m (32ft 6in)

	Di Giussano	Da Barbiano	Colleoni	Bande Nere
The following figures are calculated values based on displacement (from the registration books)	7764t	7008t	7008t	8002t
Draught (full load) forward	5.84m	5.25m	5.25m	5.87m
Draught (full load) aft	5.72m	5.41m	5.41m	5.92m
Immersed surface area of midship section	73.0m²	?	66.6m²	?
Area at waterline level	1794m²	1794m²	1768m²	1788m²
Immersed hull volume	7611m³	7706m³	6831m³	7388m³
Surface area of immersed hull	3100m³	2912m²	2844m²	2960m²
Midship section coefficient	0.82	0.81	0.80	0.79
Prismatic coefficient	0.69	0.69	0.68	0.71
Block coefficient	0.51	0.50	0.48	0.52

Displacements (figures rounded off, as in 1940)

	Di Giussano	Da Barbiano	Colleoni	Bande Nere
Ship empty and dry	5280t	5328t	5184t	5598t
Ship with full load, excluding mines	7860t	7908t	7670t	8040t
With mines	7972t	8011t	7782t	8152t

Weight breakdown, light ship

	Di Giussano	Da Barbiano	Colleoni	Bande Nere
Hull	1674t	1675t	1678t	1763t
Protection	562t	562t	562t	560t
Fittings	799t	778t	802t	836t
Machinery	1280t	1355t	1330t	1203t
Armament	508t	505t	510t	483t
Mobile weights, complement and various	225t	231t	240t	228t

Approximate weights of major stores

Fuel oil and reserve boiler water, oil, petrol	1130t
Water in boilers, donkey boilers, condensors, distiller	92
Machinery spares	10
Fixed stores	30
Consumable stores	10
Seaplanes	2
Anti-mine equipment, fog generators	7
Boats	20
Anchors, cables, warps	63
Ammunition, torpedoes, mines	292
Crew, clothing, provisions, wine, drinking water, washing water	206

MACHINERY

6 Yarrow-Ansaldo water-tube boilers with superheaters
2 groups of Belluzzo turbines with reduction gearing
2 three-bladed screws
Maximum power approximately 100,000shp
Maximum speed approximately 38kts (maximum speed of *Da Barbiano* on trials 42.05kts, developing 123,479shp)
Maximum fuel oil stowage 1290 tons (1240 useable)
Range 3800 miles at 18kts, 970 miles at 38kts

ARMAMENT

As completed

8 Ansaldo 152mm/53cal guns (in four twin turrets)
6 RM OTO 100mm/47cal guns (in three twin mountings)
2 Vickers 40mm/39cal (2pdr) automatic guns (single)
8 Terni 13.2mm machine guns (in four twin mountings)
4 torpedo tubes (533mm, in twin mountings)
2 depth charge throwers
1 catapault and 2 seaplanes
Minelaying equipment

1940–1941 (variations)

8 20mm/65cal machine guns in twin mountings (replacing the 40mm/39 guns)

PROTECTION

Belt 24–18mm
Transverse armour 20mm
Internal splinter-guard bulkheads 20mm
Second deck 20mm
Platform 12mm
Conning tower and armoured trunk 40mm
Main armament turrets 22mm

CREW

21 officers
500 non-commissioned officers and ratings (approx)

---

conning tower; many crew were killed, damage was severe, and many fires broke out. The speed of the ship dropped rapidly and soon the British destroyers could reach her with their salvoes. Shells struck the boiler room containing boilers 5 and 6, putting them out of action, and destroying the main steam collector. This damage left all the other boilers starved of water and the ship immediately stopped. Deprived of motive power, the *Colleoni* continued to fire with her 100mm guns, which could be operated manually, as long as

their reserves of ammunition lasted. All the British ships could now fire at the target, causing further devastation and fires. At 0830, six minutes after receiving the first hit, the *Colleoni* was reduced to a wreck, and the commanding officer gave the order for the survivors to abandon ship.

At that moment, from short range, the *Ilex* and the *Havock* launched torpedoes at the *Colleoni*, the first of which struck slightly forward of the forward turret, causing about thirty metres of hull to become detached and sink. The second struck the ship amidships, opening a large hole through which water flooded in, causing her to capsize and sink rapidly, with the stern slightly out of the water.

While the *Sidney*, *Hero* and *Hasty* moved away, following the *Bande Nere*, the *Havock*, *Ilex* and *Hyperion* steamed to the point where the ship had sunk, and lowered scrambling netting to recover the survivors; 525 were rescued, of which 93 were wounded; 8 of them did not survive and were buried at sea, with military honours, off Alexandria. A further 4 died soon after their arrival in port, amongst them the commanding officer of the *Colleoni*, Captain Umberto Novaro who, gravely wounded, had been assisted by an officer of the *Ilex* since being taken on board. Commander Novaro was buried with full honours, as were the other dead. The funerals took place at Alexandria, in the presence of British officers and sailors from the ships which had taken part in the action; Captain Collins of the *Sidney* and the commanders of the other English ships bore the coffins.

Not all the survivors sought salvation on board the British ships; about fifty, it seems, tried to swim to the nearby coast, but only seven succeeded in their attempt, when they were picked up by a Greek fishing boat. The British destroyers would probably have picked up a greater number of survivors if it had not been for a number of Italian bombers from Rhodes which arrived on the scene soon after. They dropped bombs on the British ships, causing no more than minor damage to the *Havock*, but forcing the vessels to move away, and hence suspend the rescue operations. Thus the only result of the bombing was that the number of deaths from the sinking was greater than necessary. Of the 643 men on the *Colleoni*, 4 officers, 17 non-commissioned officers and 100 petty officers and sailors died that day.

The duel between the *Bande Nere* and the ships pursuing her continued until 0926, when the *Sidney*, outdistanced by the faster Italian cruiser, altered course to starboard and left the scene, followed by two destroyers which were escorting her: the *Sidney* only had four rounds remaining for A turret and one for B turret (during this phase of the combat the *Sidney* was only using her forward turrets). During this final phase of the encounter the *Bande Nere* was hit by one 6in (152mm) shell, but without serious consequences.

The Photographs

2. Ansaldo yard at Genoa Sestri, June 1928: after the ceremonial laying of the first plate, the keel plates are installed on 'ship No 288' on the slips.

Ansaldo archive

3. Ansaldo yard at Genoa Sestri, August 1928: the hull has been built up to the battery deck (first level) and main deck (second level).

Ansaldo archive

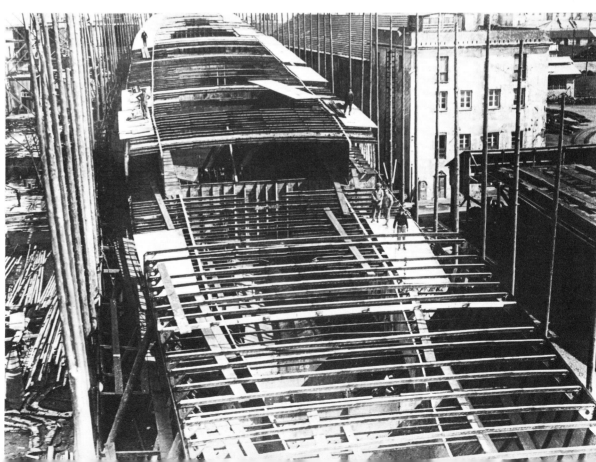

6

4. Ansaldo yard at Genoa Sestri, 30 September 1928: the hull of the *Bartolomeo Colleoni* after three months' work.

Bargoni Collection

5. The *Bartolomeo Colleoni* on the slips of the Ansaldo yard a few days before launch.

Bargoni Collection

6. This photograph of the *Alberico da Barbiano*, the *Colleoni*'s twin, taken on the day of launching, clearly shows the barbettes for the two 152mm forward turrets, the position of the seaplane catapult, and the position of the tracks for transferring the aircraft from the hangar to the catapult, indicated by white stripes on the deck.

Bargoni Collection

7. Another photo of the *Alberico da Barbiano* on the day of launching. As well as the barbettes for the after turrets (one is covered by planking), the after wheelhouse and the tripod main mast can be seen – two structures which were soon reduced in size in an effort to improve the ship's stability. Note the launch ways which extend under the sea's surface, covered with tallow for reducing friction and aiding the launch. The fishing boats mirrored in the sea off the slipway are waiting to pick up pieces of tallow, which will float to the surface after the launch.

Bargoni Collection

7

8

8. Taranto, 2 October 1933: the *Bartolomeo Colleoni* leaves the navigable channel. The rangefinder on the after wheelhouse is still in place.

Bargoni Collection

9. Forward superstructure of the cruiser *Bartolomeo Colleoni*. From the top: the main fire control director, the command bridge, the second fire control director, the rangefinder on the roof of Turret 2. The bas-relief portrait of Bartolomeo Colleoni can be made out on the gun tompions.

Bargoni Collection

10. The *Colleoni* entering the Taranto navigable channel. *Bargoni Collection*

11. The two cruisers *Bartolomeo Colleoni* (left) and the *Alberto di Giussano* in the Ferrati basin at Taranto, for cleaning the underwater hull.

Bargoni Collection

12. The same cruisers photographed a few days later in the careening basin.

Bargoni Collection

13. The *Colleoni* at anchor, photographed in April 1934.

Aldo Fraccaroli

14. The *Colleoni* at Mar Grande, Taranto in 1935.

Bargoni Collection

15. The *Colleoni* on a mooring at La Spezia in 1937, having returned from a mission in Spanish waters.

Bargoni Collection

16. Naples, 5 May 1938: Naval Review 'H' in honour of the German Chancellor Adolf Hitler. The *Colleoni* is passing the official ship with the crew lining the side.

Bargoni Collection

17. The *Colleoni* leaving the port of Genoa, 30 May 1938.

Bargoni Collection

18. In 1938 the *Colleoni* was despatched to Shanghai to protect the Italian legation. In the months of March–April 1939 she completed a cruise calling at various Northern Chinese and Japanese ports. In the photograph the ship is at Yokohama.

Bargoni Collection

19. Detail of the IMAM Ro 43 reconnaissance floatplane.

Author's Collection

20. The *Bande Nere*'s seaplane, slightly damaged by shell-fire, after the encounter at Cape Spada. The number indicates that it belongs to II Division (2), to the first unit of the division (1) and is the ship's second aircraft (2).

Author's Collection

21–24. Battle of Cape Spada, 19 July 1940: the two ships of II Division, *Giovanni dalle Bande Nere* and *Bartolomeo Colleoni*, have sighted the enemy and are increasing speed, producing prodigious quantities of smoke. In photo 21 the *Colleoni* is seen astern of the *Bande Nere*.

Bargoni Collection

21

22. Cape Spada: the *Colleoni* at high speed.

Bargoni Collection

23, 24. Two views of the *Colleoni* dead in the water with the bow missing; taken from the British destroyers as they closed in to pick up the *Colleoni*'s crew.

Imperial War Museum

The Drawings

A General arrangements

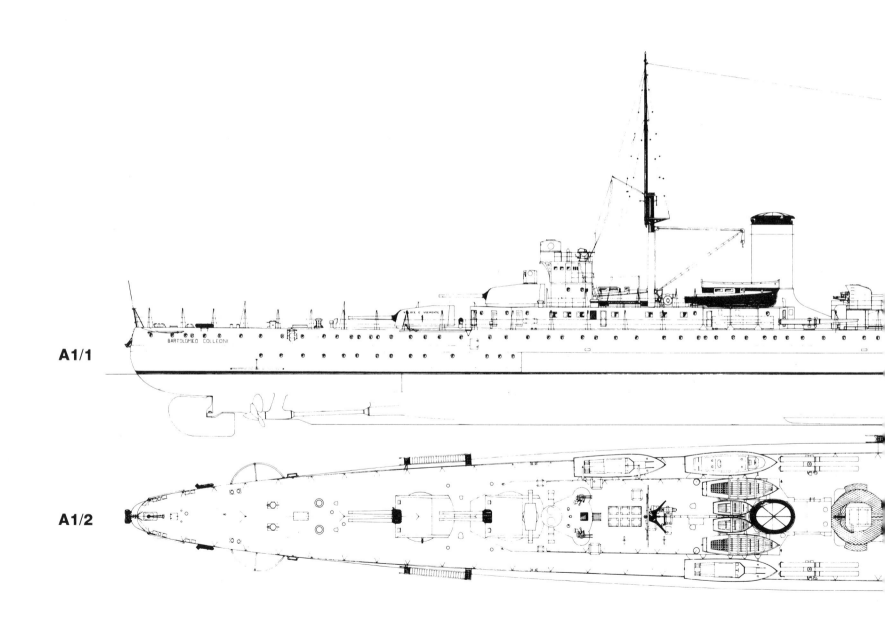

A1/1

A1/2

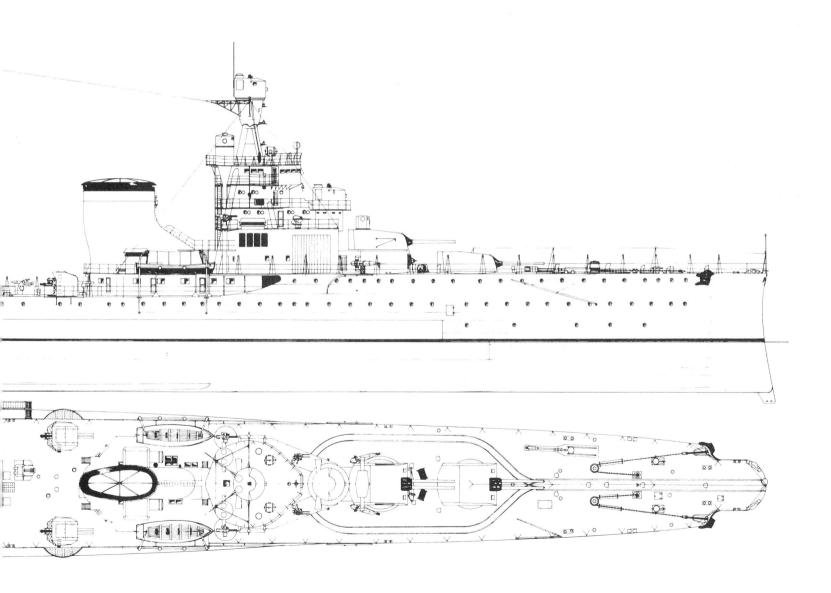

A General arrangements

A2/1 Internal profile

1 Stern anchor hawsepipe
2 Quartermaster's store
3 Quartermaster's store entrance
4 Officer's bath and WC
5 Officers' baggage store
6 Steering gear compartment
7 Officers' cabins
8 Admiral's and captain's cellar and pantry
9 After peak
10 Access to steering gear compartment
11 After capstan drum
12 Steering gear machinery space
13 Ballast tank
14 Fuel oil (from April 1939 boiler feed water)
15 After bilge pump room

16 Turret 4 trunk
17 After magazine
18 Paymaster's secretary's office
19 Ammunition loading scuttle
20 Cage hoist
21 Refrigeration space
22 Fuel oil
23 Guardhouse
24 Turret 3 trunk
25 Base of 5m rangefinder
26 After conning position
27 Gunnery secretary's office (from 1933 radio receiver room)
28 Admiral's secretary's office (from 1933 divisional secretary's office)
29 Pantry
30 Briefing room
31 Crew accommodation

32 Main radio room entrance
33 Dynamo room
34 After engine room (port propeller shaft)
35 Base for turbines, condensor and reduction gearing
36 Lubricating oil gathering tank
37 Grating deck
38 Light grills
39 Engine room skylight
40 Armoured grating of engine room skylight
41 Derrick
42 Boat chock
43 Captain's cabin
44 Officer's galley
45 Engineering office
46 Boiler 6 uptake

47 Boiler 5 uptake
48 Air trunk to after boiler room (5 and 6)
49 Ventilator for after boiler room
50 Hatch and companionway
51 After boiler room (5 and 6)
52 Forge and smelting furnace
53 Auxiliary boiler
54 Access to dynamo room
55 Support for 100mm/47 gun
56 Platform for 100mm/47 gun
57 Armoured grating of engine room skylight
58 Forward engine room (starboard propeller shaft)
59 Loading trainer
60 Engineering workshop
61 Small arms magazine
62 Access to midships magazine

A2/1

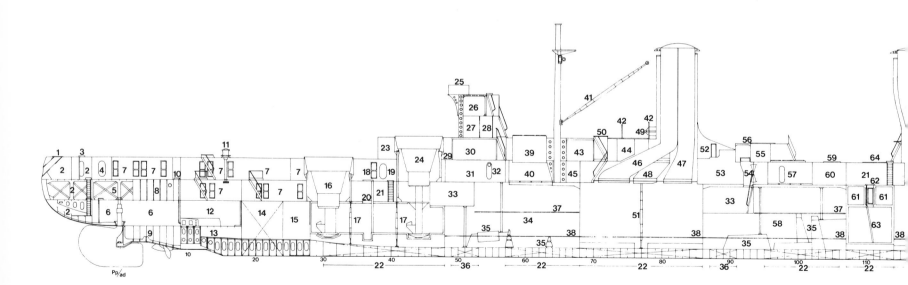

63	Midships magazine	80	Cipher office	97	Turret 1	114	Non-commissioned officers'
64	Base for 100mm/47 gun	81	Officers' library (from April 1939	98	Meat store		baggage store
65	Boiler 4 uptake		naval-air radio room)	99	Forward bilge pump room	115	Aviation fuel stowage
66	Boiler 3 uptake	82	Gunnery secretary's office	100	Fuel tank for motor boats	116	Fore peak
67	Air trunk to central boiler room (3 and	83	Conning tower	101	Access to pump room	117	Access to fore peak
	4)	84	Hangar for two seaplanes	102	Boiler reserve feed water		
68	Central boiler room	85	Hangar doors	103	Capstan		
69	Boiler 2 uptake	86	Linen store	104	Pantry		
70	Boiler 1 uptake	87	Clothes pressing room	105	Navel pipes		
71	Air trunk to forward boilers (1 and 2)	88	Battery store	106	Flour store		
72	Forward boiler room (1 and 1)	89	Mail office	107	'Spalazzi' log room		
73	Main gun director (Director I)	90	Transmitting station	108	Wine store		
74	3m rangefinder	91	Master gyro compass room	109	Chain locker		
75	Charthouse	92	Torpedo warhead magazine	110	Access to chain locker		
76	Wheelhouse	93	Turret 2	111	Access to aviation fuel stowage		
77	Captain's cabin	94	Forward magazine	112	Crew WCs		
78	WC and wash place	95	Main fire control gear	113	Crew wash place		
79	Armoured gun director (Director II)	96	Access to forward magazine				

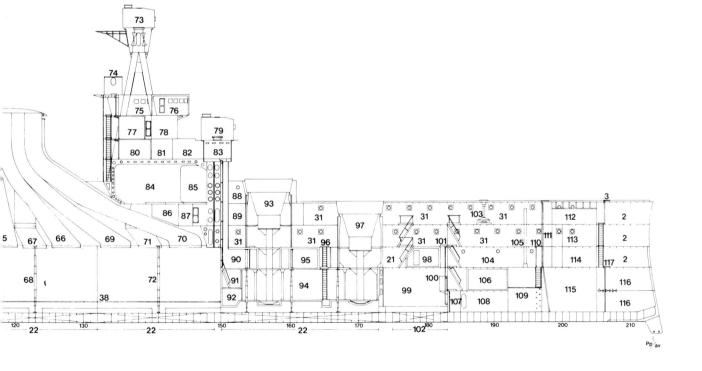

A General arrangements

A2/2 Section at frame 8 looking forward
1 Officers' quarters
2 Access to officers' baggage store
3 Officers' baggage store
4 Cellar and pantry for admiral and captain
5 Officers' cellar and pantry
6 Access to steering gear compartment
7 Steering gear compartment
8 After peak

A2/3 Section at frame 37 looking aft
1 Accountant's cabin
2 Paymaster's secretary's office
3 Turret 3 base
4 Ammunition hoist
5 Crew accommodation
6 After magazine
7 Fuel oil
8 Shaft tunnel
9 Double bottom

A2/4 Section at frame 62 looking aft
1 After fire control position
2 After conning position
3 Admiral's secretary's office (from 1933 divisional secretary's office)
4 Flag lieutenant's cabin
5 Secretary's office
6 Chock for admiral's barge
7 Engine room skylight
8 Accommodation for seven chief petty officers
9 Crew accommodation
10 After engine room
11 Petty officers' mess and galley
12 Chief quartermaster's store
13 Boiler feed water
14 Longitudinal bulkhead
15 Fuel oil

A2/5 Section of frame 75
1 After funnel
2 Chocks for motor launches
3 Chocks for 4.5m pulling boats
4 Chock for 10m diesel launch
5 Chock for 10m fast motor boat
6 Boiler 6 uptake
7 Officers' galley
8 Admiral's and captain's galley
9 Reserve torpedoes
10 Petty officers' mess
11 Chief petty officers' wash place
12 After boiler room (boilers 5 and 6)
13 Torpedo storekeeper (from September 1938 ballast tank 3)
14 Galley for chief petty officers' mess (from September 1938 ballast tank 4)
15 Boiler reserve feed water
16 Cofferdams
17 Fuel oil

A2/6 Section at frame 98 looking aft
1 After funnel
2 After superstructure
3 Ventilator for forward boiler room
4 Platform for 100mm/47 gun
5 Accommodation for eleven petty officers (from September 1938 crew wash and shower room)
6 Crew accommodation
7 Skylight for engine room
8 Forward engine room (starboard propeller shaft)
9 Gunnery storekeeper's store
10 Seaplane equipment
11 Lubricating oil
12 Washing water
13 Longitudinal bulkhead
14 Fuel oil

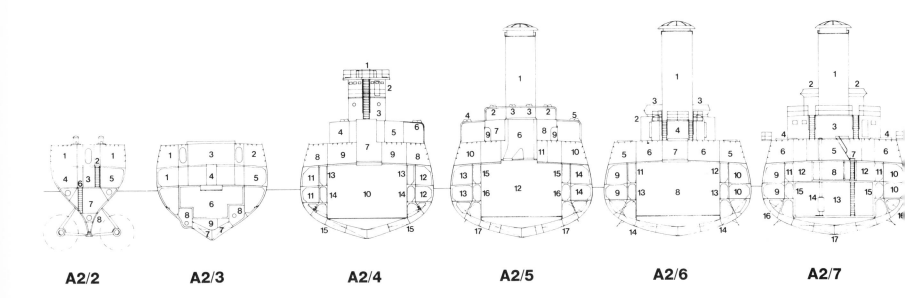

A2/2   **A2/3**   **A2/4**   **A2/5**   **A2/6**   **A2/7**

A2/7	**Section at frame 110 looking forward**	A2/8	**Section at frame 139 looking aft**	A2/9	**Section at frame 152 looking aft**	A2/10	**Section at frame 163 looking aft**

A2/7 **Section at frame 110 looking forward**
1 Forward funnel
2 Ventilator for central boiler room
3 Forecastle
4 Base for 100mm/47 guns
5 Refrigeration machinery
6 Accommodation for five petty officers
7 Access to central magazine
8 Small arms magazine
9 Store
10 Clothing store
11 Washing water
12 Pipework trunking
13 Central magazine
14 Ammunition hoist
15 Longitudinal bulkhead
16 lubricating oil
17 Fuel oil

A2/8 **Section at frame 139 looking aft**
1 Base of 3m rangefinder
2 Charthouse
3 Captain's cabin
4 Admiral's cabin
5 Cipher office
6 Radio room
7 Hangar for two seaplanes
8 Air trunk to forward boiler room
9 Boiler 2 uptake
10 Pantry
11 Crew WCs and showers
12 Stokers' wash place
13 Forward boiler room (boilers 1 and 2)
14 Adjutant's store (from September 1938 oakum store)
15 Aviation storekeeper's store
16 Wash place
17 Longitudinal bulkhead
18 Fuel oil

A2/9 **Section at frame 152 looking aft**
1 Searchlight platform
2 Bridge and wheelhouse
3 Armoured director platform
4 Conning tower
5 Ventilator for forward boiler room
6 Armoured access to transmitting station
7 Hangar doors
8 Ship's hospital
9 Isolation ward
10 Mail office
11 Crew accommodation
12 Cable trunking – radio room
13 Transmitting station
14 Tactical plot
15 Medium wave radio room
16 Workshop 'A'
17 Workshop 'B'
18 Gyro compass
19 Pump and converter
20 Master gyro compass room
21 Electrician's store
22 Torpedo warhead magazine
23 Fuel oil

A2/10 **Section at frame 163 looking aft**
1 Turret 2
2 Crew accommodation
3 Dynamo and fire control switchgear
4 Forward magazine
5 Clothing store
6 Bed linen store (from September 1939 electrician's store)
7 Fuel oil

A2/11 **Section at frame 180 looking forward**
1 Capstan machinery
2 Crew accommodation
3 Vegetable refrigerator
4 Meat refrigerator
5 Bilge pump room
6 Boiler reserve feed water

A2/12 **Section at frame 200 looking forward**
1 Crew WCs
2 Crew WCs
3 Crew accommodation
4 Quartermaster's store
5 Aviation fuel

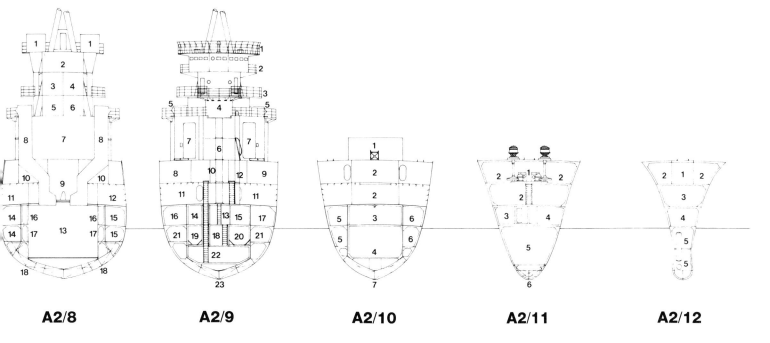

A2/8   **A2/9**   **A2/10**   **A2/11**   **A2/12**

A General arrangements

A3 DECKS (all 1/400 scale)

A3/1 After superstructure
1 Turret 3 barbette
2 Gunnery secretary's office
3 Admiral's secretary's office
4 Ventilator for after engine room
5 Skylight for after engine room
6 Boat chocks
7 Windlass
8 Support for 10m fast motor boat
9 Cowl ventilators
10 Support for 10m barge
11 Galley skylight
12 Chocks for 8.6m boats
13 Chocks for 4.5m boats
14 Ventilators for after boiler room
15 Base for 13.2mm machine guns (from Summer 1940)
16 Boiler casing
17 Platform for 100mm/47 gun
18 Base for 100mm/47 gun

A3/2 After conning position
1 Wheelhouse
2 Hatchway
3 Base of steering gear

A3/3 After fire control platform
1 Base of 5m rangefinder
2 Base of navigational instruments
3 Base of 13.2mm machine guns
4 Access to platform

A3/4 Forecastle deck
1 Skylight for petty officer's galley
2 Skylight for hospital galley
3 Short wave radio room
4 Ventilator for central boiler room
5 Water tank
6 Galley chimneys
7 Skylight for crew galley
8 Chocks for 8.6m boat
9 Davits for 8.6m boat
10 Skylights to bakery and laundry
11 Shaft for air conditioning installation
12 Discharge for air conditioning installation
13 Base for 40mm guns
14 Seaplane hangar
15 Ventilation shaft to forward boiler room
16 Turntable platform
17 Hangar doors
18 Battery store
19 Seaplane rails
20 Water hydrant (for fire-fighting and washing down decks)
21 Turret 2 barbette
22 Paravanes
23 Ventilators
24 Turret 1 barbette
25 Seaplane derrick
26 Catapult track
27 Cowl ventilator
28 Catapult cradle
29 Capstan
30 Chain stoppers
31 Bollards
32 Catapult rails
33 Hatch to aviation fuel store
34 Hawse pipes
35 Hatch to quartermaster's store

A3/5 Hangar
1 Companionway
2 Ventilation to forward boiler room
3 Hangar doors
4 Hangar space for two seaplanes

A3/6 Machine gun platform (conning tower level)
1 Base for 40mm guns
2 Base for 13.2mm guns
3 Ventilation trunks for forward boiler room
4 Navigation lights
5 Radio room
6 Cipher office
7 Officers' library (from April 1939 Naval-Air radio room)
8 Gunnery secretary's office
9 Conning tower
10 Base of steering instruments
11 Hatch to transmitting station

A3/7 Armoured director platform
1 Support for 3m rangefinder
2 Base for fighting lights
3 Admiral's cabin
4 Captain's cabin
5 Signal lamps
6 WC and wash place
7 Companionway to chartroom
8 Armoured director

A3/3

A3/2

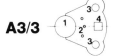

A3/1

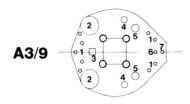

A3/9

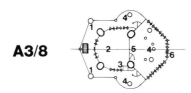

A3/8

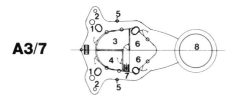

A3/7

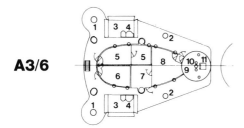

A3/6

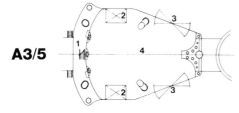

A3/5

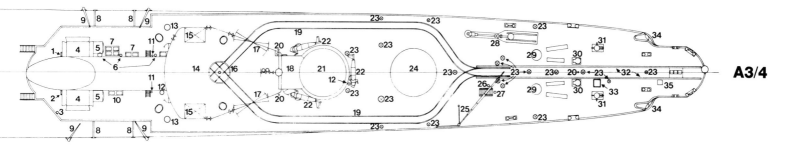

A3/4

A3/8 Bridge deck
1   Support for 3m rangefinder
2   Chartroom
3   Companionway to admiral's and
     captain's cabins
4   Bases of navigation instruments
5   Wheelhouse
6   Clear vision glass

A3/9 Searchlight platform
1   Base of look-out positions
2   Base of 3m rangfinder
3   Companionway to bridge deck
4   Base of 13.2mm guns
5   Base of 90cm searchlights
6   Compass
7   Radio direction finder antenna

A General arrangements

A3/10 Upper deck

1	Anchor (2000kg)
2	Stern anchor hawsepipe
3	Hatch to quartermaster's store
4	Filler cap for drinking water tank
5	Filler cap for washing water tank
6	Ventilators
7	Water hydrant (fire-fighting and washing down decks)
8	'Stern clear' signal light
9	After capstans
10	Turret 4 barbette
11	Guardhouse
12	Turret 3 barbette
13	Pantry
14	Admiral's bathroom
15	Admiral's sleeping cabin
16	Admiral's day cabin
17	Briefing room
18	Secretary's office
19	Records secretary's office
20	Skylight to after engine room
21	Flag lieutenant's cabin
22	Captain's day cabin
23	Captain's sleeping cabin
24	Captain's bathroom
25	Chief of staff's day cabin
26	Chief of staff's sleeping cabin
27	Chief of staff's bathroom
28	Officers' galley
29	Admiral's and captain's galley
30	Boilers 5 and 6 uptakes
31	Spare torpedo stowage
32	Forge
33	Bases of torpedo tubes
34	Personnel secretary's office
35	Skylight to dynamo and auxiliary boiler
36	Filler cap to drinking water tank
37	Filler cap to washing water tank
38	Base of 100mm/47 gun platform
39	Skylight to forward engine room
40	Loading trainer
41	Cage hoists for 100mm/47 guns
42	Bases of 100mm/47 guns
43	Petty officers' galley
44	Hospital galley
45	Boiler uptakes
46	Crew's galley
47	Bakery
48	Laundry
49	Storekeepers' galley
50	Closet
51	Linen store
52	Clothes pressing room
53	Barber
54	First aid post
55	Sick bay attendant
56	Decontamination chamber
57	Isolation ward (four-bed)
58	Bathroom and WC for isolation wards
59	Ship's hospital (seven-bed)
60	Hospital bathroom and WC
61	Pharmacy
62	Mail office
63	100mm/47 ready-use ammunition
64	Turret 2 barbette
65	Turret 1 barbette
66	Crew accommodation
67	Capstan machinery
68	Hatch to aviation fuel store
69	Crew WCs
70	Crew WCs
71	Hatch to quartermaster's store
72	Quartermaster's store

A3/10

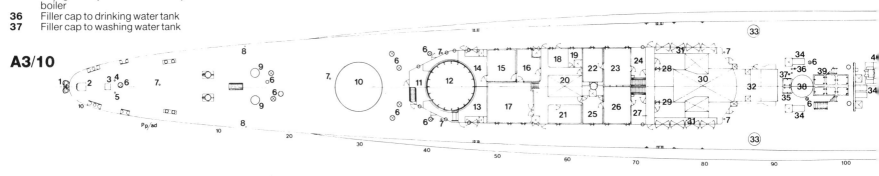

A3/11

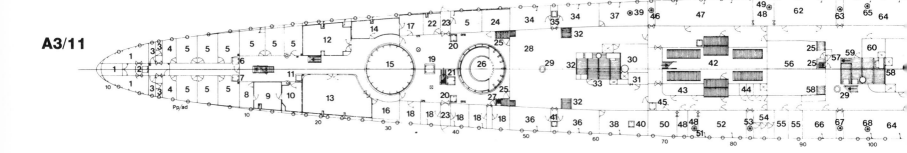

A3/11 Lower deck

1 Quartermaster's store
2 Access to quartermaster's store
3 Officer's WC
4 Officers' bathrooms
5 Officers' cabins
6 Hatch to steering gear compartment
7 Hatch to officer's baggage store
8 Exececutive officer's bathroom and WC
9 Executive officer's cabin
10 Executive officer's day cabin
11 Hatch to the steering gear machinery room
12 Wardroom annexe
13 Wardroom
14 Engineering commander's cabin
15 Turret 4 barbette
16 Officers' cellar and pantry
17 Engineering commander's bathroom and WC
18 Accountant's cabin
19 Cage hoist
20 Hatch to shaft tunnel
21 Access to after magazine
22 Paymaster's secretarys' office
23 Ammunition loading passages
24 Supernumerary officer's cabin
25 Skylight to turbo dynamo room
26 Turret 3 barbette
27 Access to turbo dynamo room
28 Crew accommodation
29 Base of fuel oil filter

30 Engineering office
31 Engine spares
32 Skylight to after engine room
33 Access to after engine room
34 Cabins for six chief petty officers
35 Hatch to main radio compartment
36 Cabins for six chief petty officers
37 Cabin for seven chief petty officers
38 Cabin for seven chief petty officers
39 Access to aviation store
40 Hatch to chief petty officers' mess store (pantry)
41 Hatch to mechanician's store
42 Boilers 5 and 6 uptakes
43 Chief petty officer's wash place
44 Chief petty officer's showers
45 Hatch to boiler room
46 Access to torpedo store
47 Chief petty officers' mess
48 Chief petty officer's mess pantry
49 Petty officers' pantry entrance
50 Storekeepers' mess
51 Storekeepers' pantry entrance
52 Chief petty officers' mess
53 Hatch to torpedo store
54 Storekeepers' and chief petty officers' WC
55 Storekeepers' and chief petty officers' bathrooms
56 Auxiliary boiler room
57 Access to auxiliary boiler room
58 Skylight to forward engine room
59 Access to forward engine room

60 Engine control room
61 Engineering workshop
62 Chief petty officers' mess
63 Access to mechanicians's store
64 Cabin for eleven chief petty officers
65 Access to seaplane equipment store
66 Cabin for five chief petty officers
67 Access to mechanician's store
68 Access to gunnery store
69 Hatch to small arms magazine
70 Cage ammunition hoist
71 Crew wash places
72 Boilers 3 and 4 uptakes
73 Hatch to boiler room
74 Engineering workshops
75 Access to compressor room
76 Petty officers' WCs
77 Petty officers' wash place and showers
78 Access to torpedo store
79 Access to oakum store
80 Stokers' wash place and showers
81 Cabin for four civilians
82 Access to spare store
83 Hatch to short wave radio compartment
84 Hatch to boiler room
85 Boilers 1 and 2 uptakes
86 Crew wash place and showers
87 Hatch to carpenter's store
88 Crew WCs
89 Canteen
90 Access to master at arms' store

91 Crew WCs
92 Prison
93 Transmitting station access trunk
94 Access to torpedo warhead magazine
95 Hatch to workshop 'E'
96 Hatch to workshop 'A'
97 Access to bedding store
98 Access to clothing store
99 Access to dynamo and main fire control switchgear room
100 Cage ammunition hoist
101 Hatch to magazine
102 Turret 2 barbette
103 Access to transmitting station
104 Turret 1 barbette
105 Access to refrigeration equipment
106 Ports for ammunition loading
107 Hatch to stabiliser room
108 Access to pantry
109 Access to non-commissioned officers' baggage room
110 Aviation fuel store access

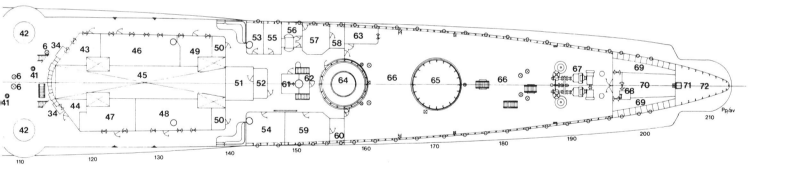

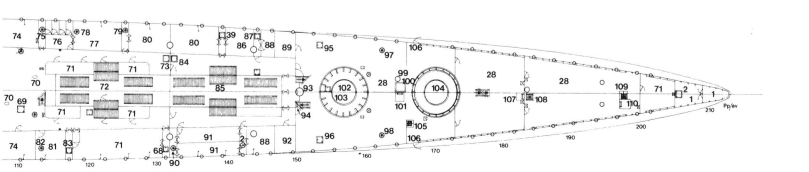

A General arrangements

A3/12 Platform deck

1 Quartermaster's store
2 Hatch to steering gear compartment
3 Officers' baggage store
4 Admiral's and captain's cellar (wine and spirits store)
5 Admiral's and captain's pantry
6 Officers' mess cellar
7 Officers' mess pantry
8 Capstan machinery
9 Officers' cabins
10 Naval ordnance lieutenant's cabin
11 Naval ordnance officer's cabin
12 Orderly's room
13 Base for hand steering gear
14 Compass base
15 Hatch to bilge pump room
16 Observer officer's cabin
17 Cabin for two midshipmen
18 Navigating officer's cabin
19 Engineering officer's cabin
20 Cage ammunition hoist
21 Access to magazine
22 Access to shaft tunnel
23 Turret 4 barbette
24 Turret 3 barbette
25 Crew accommodation
26 Storekeepers' cabin
27 Master at arms' cabin
28 Tailor and shoemaker
29 Cabin for two non-commissioned officers
30 WC
31 Dynamo room

32 After engine room (port propeller shaft)
33 Main radio compartment
34 Mechanician's store
35 Drinking water
36 Helmsman's store
37 Chief petty officers' mess pantry
38 Boiler feed water
39 Boiler room (boilers 5 and 6)
40 Access to boiler room
41 Torpedo gear store
42 Storekeepers mess pantry
43 Petty officers' mess pantry
44 Torpedo gear store
45 Boiler reserve feed water
46 Forward engine room (starboard propeller shaft)
47 Mechanician's store
48 Seaplane gear store
49 Ordnance gear store
50 Fuel oil
51 Washing water
52 Lubrication oil
53 Small arms magazine
54 Access to magazine
55 Cage ammunition hoist
56 Steam pipes conduit
57 Reciprocating compressor
58 Boiler room (boilers 3 and 4)
59 Access to boiler room
60 Short wave radio compartment
61 Oakum store
62 Boiler room (boilers 1 and 2)
63 Access to boiler room

64 Master at arms' store
65 Carpenter's store
66 Transmitting station
67 Radio room
68 Access to master gyro compass compartment
69 Hatch to torpedo warhead magazine
70 Turret 2 barbette
71 Central fire control equipment compartment
72 Cage ammunition hoist
73 Access to magazine
74 Electrician's workshop
75 Ordnance workshop
76 Clothing store
77 Bedding store
78 Refrigeration equipment
79 Turret 1 barbette
80 Ice box
81 Deep freeze compartment
82 Access to stabilizer compartment
83 Pantry
84 Non-commissioned officers' baggage store
85 Access to aviation fuel store

A3/12

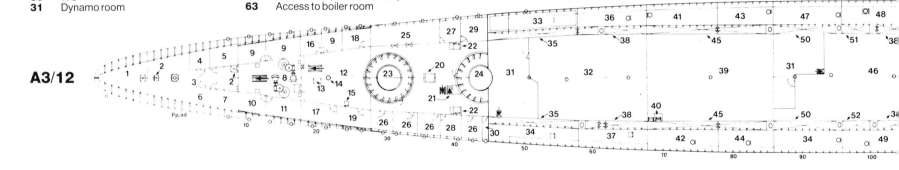

A3/13

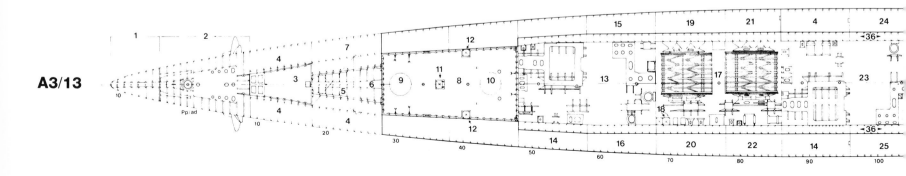

A3/13 Hold

1	Quartermaster's store
2	Steering gear compartment
3	Steering machinery
4	Mechanician's store – damage control equipment
5	Fuel oil
6	After bilge pump room
7	Sickbay attendant's store
8	After magazine
9	Base of Turret 4
10	Base of Turret 3
11	Cage ammunition hoist
12	Well access to shaft tunnels
13	After engine room
14	Mechanian's store
15	Helmsman's store
16	Chief petty officers' store
17	Boiler room (boilers 5 and 6)
18	Access to boiler room
19	Torpedo gear store
20	Storekeepers' mess pantry
21	Petty officers' mess pantry
22	Torpedo gear store
23	Forward engine room
24	Seaplane gear store
25	Ordnance store
26	Central magazine
27	Base of cage hoist
28	Bedding store
29	Clothing store
30	Boiler room (boilers 3 and 4)
31	Access to boiler room
32	Carpenter's store
33	Boiler room (boilers 1 and 2)
34	Access to boiler room
35	Master at arms' store
36	Cofferdams (water-filled when on active service)
37	Torpedo warhead magazine
38	Forward magazine
39	Base of Turret 2
40	Base of Turret 1
41	Cage ammunition hoist
42	Electrician's store
43	Paint store
44	Forward bilge pump room
45	Motor boats' fuel tank
46	Cheese store
47	Flour store
48	'Spalazzi' log well
49	Wine store
50	Chain locker
51	Aviation fuel store
52	Fore peak

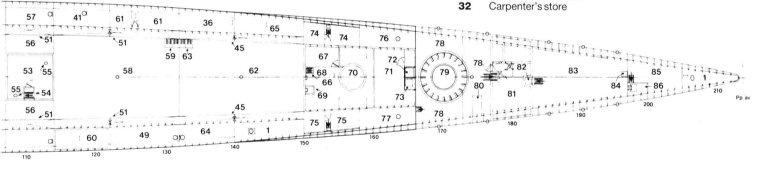

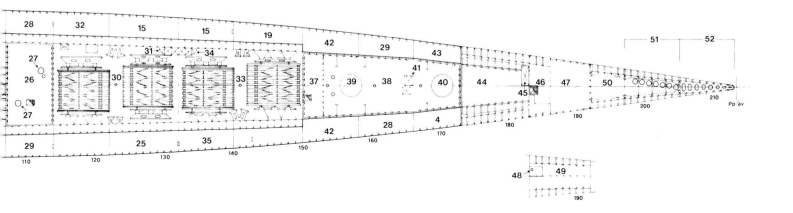

39

A General arrangements

A4/1

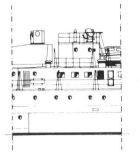

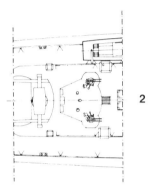

1

2

A4/2

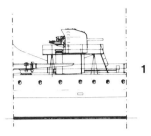

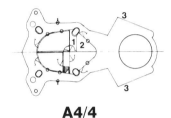

1

2

A4/3

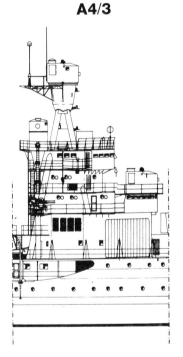

1

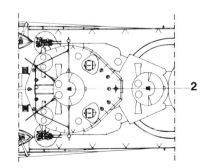

2

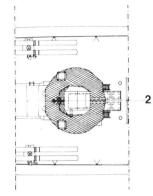

3

3

A4/4

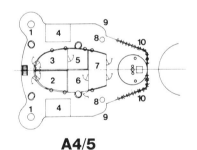

1
4
9
8
10
3 5 7
2 6
1 4
9
8
10

A4/5

A4   SUPERSTRUCTURE MODIFICATIONS (1/400 scale)

A4/1   After conning position from Winter 1933–34
1   External profile
2   Deck plan

A4/2   Midships 100mm/47 gun platform, from Winter 1933–34
1   External profile
2   Deck plan

A4/3   Forward superstructure, Summer 1940
1   External profile
2   Deck plan

A4/4   Modifications to armoured director platform, to April 1939
1   Admiral's WC (April 1939)
2   Radio direction finder station (April 1939)
3   Platform widened (Winter 1933–1934)

A4/5   Modifications to machine gun platform, to Summer 1940
1   40mm/39 gun replaced with 20mm/65 machine guns (Summer 1940)
2   Gunnery secretary's office (Winter 1933–1934)
3   Radio transmitter room (April 1939)
4   Closing-in boilers 1 and 2 air trunks (April 1939)
5   Radio signaller (April 1939)
6   Naval-Air radio (aircraft liaison communications) room (April 1939)
7   Cipher office (April 1939)
8   13.2mm machine guns removed (Summer 1940)
9   Platform extended (Winter 1933–1934)
10   Platform lowered (Winter 1933–1934)

A5/1

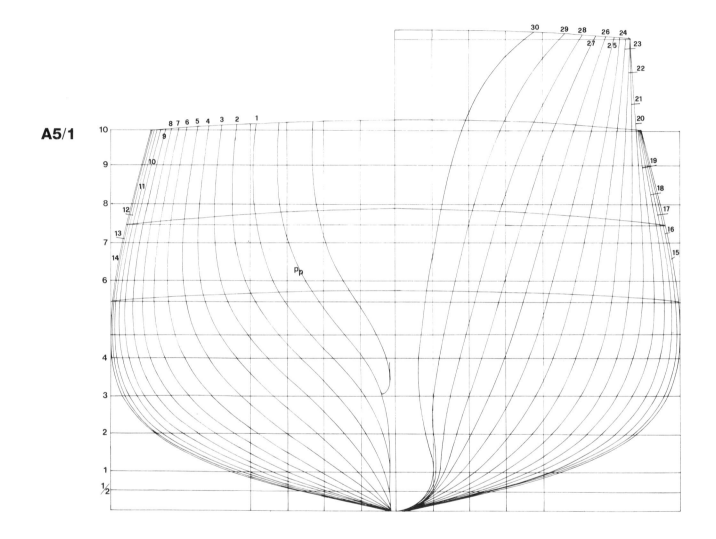

A5/2 Sheer plan (1/200 scale)

A5/2

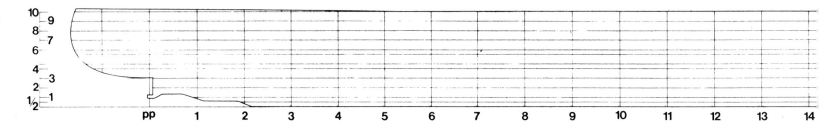

A5/4

A5/3

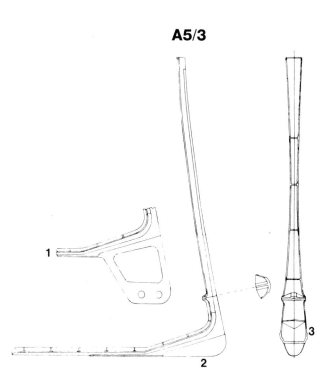

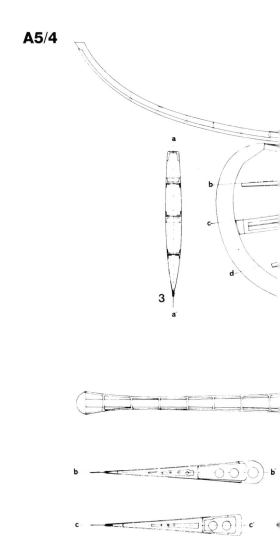

A5/3 Stem detail (1/100 scale)
1 Paravane fitting
2 Profile
3 Front view

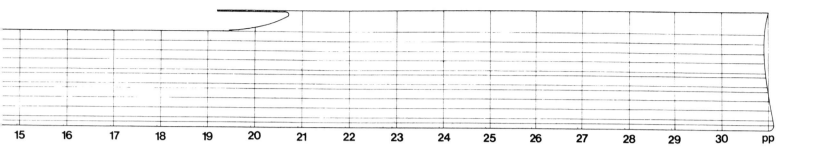

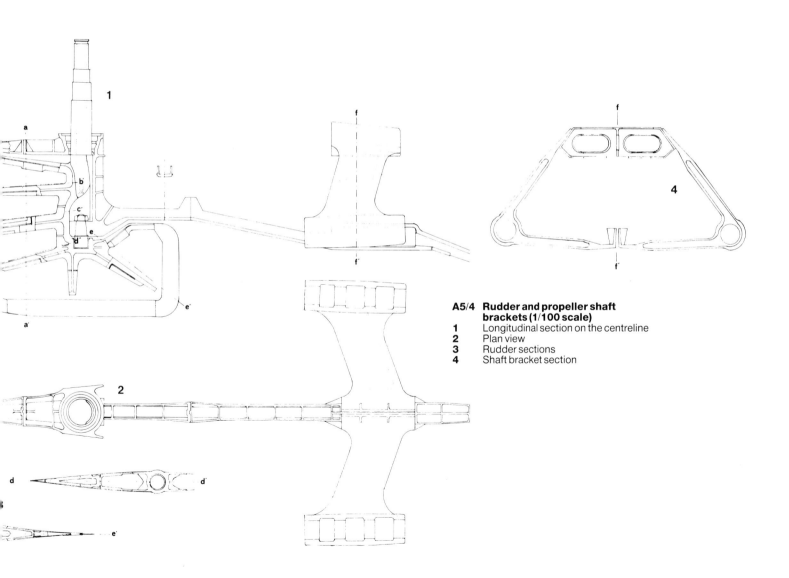

**A5/4 Rudder and propeller shaft
brackets (1/100 scale)**

1 Longitudinal section on the centreline
2 Plan view
3 Rudder sections
4 Shaft bracket section

A General arrangements

A5/5 Outer longitudinal bulkhead
(1/400 scale)
Note: Plates marked * are armour

A5/6 Inner longitudinal bulkhead
(1/400 scale)
Note: Plates marked * are armour

A5/7 Longitudinal bulkhead, portside
plan (1/400 scale)

A5/8 Plating expansion (1/400 scale)

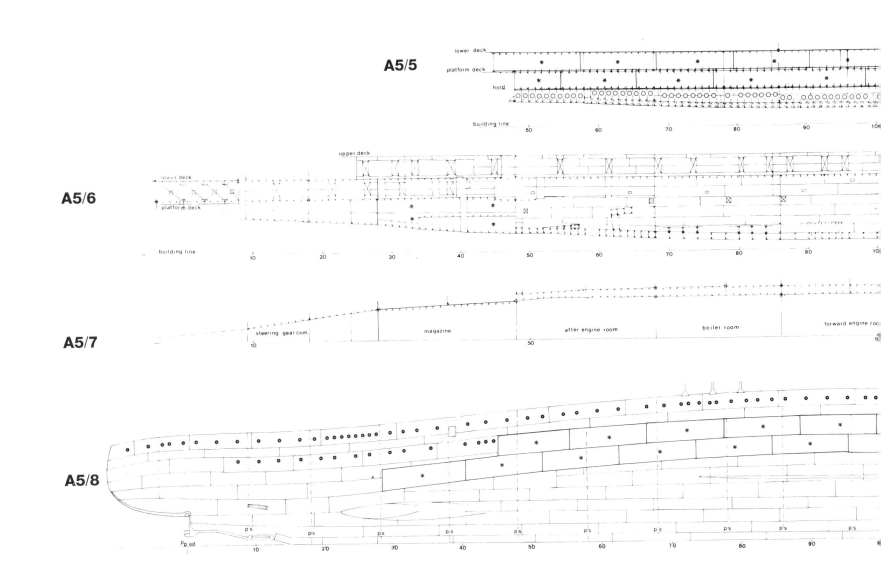

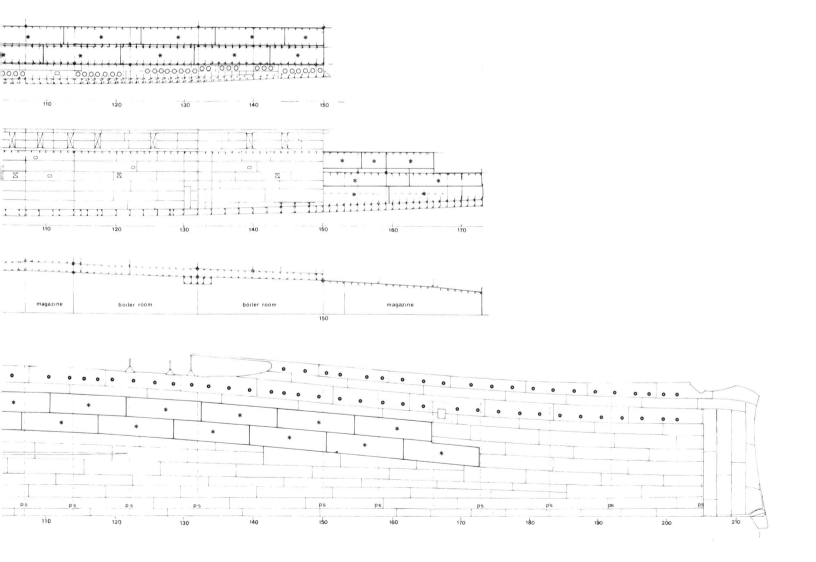

110   120   130   140   150

110   120   130   140   150   160   170

magazine   boiler room   boiler room   magazine

150

110   120   130   140   150   160   170   180   190   200   210

p.s   p.s   p.s   p.s   p.s   p.s   p.s   p.s   p.s   p.s

110   120   130   140   150   160   170   180   190   200   210

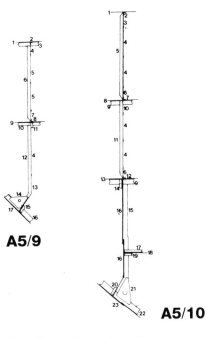

A5/9

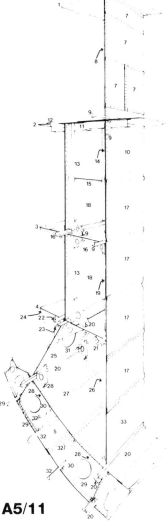

A5/10

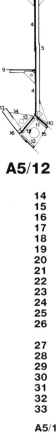

A5/11

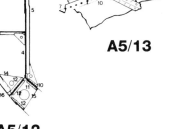

A5/12

A5/13

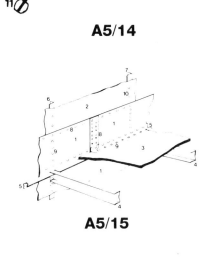

A5/14

A5/15

A5/9 Frame 21, section of inner longitudinal bulkhead (1/100 scale)
1 Lower deck
2 45mm × 45mm × 5mm angle bar
3 125mm × 63mm × 7.5mm angle bar
4 5mm longitudinal plate
5 2.5mm longitudinal plates
6 80mm × 60mm × 6mm angle bar
7 4mm longitudinal plate
8 45mm × 45mm × 5mm horizontal angle bar
9 Platform deck
10 95mm × 60mm × 7mm angle bar
11 45mm × 45mm × 7mm vertical angle bar
12 80mm × 45mm × 6mm × 8mm 'C' bar
13 6mm longitudinal plate
14 5mm bracket
15 60mm × 60mm × 6mm angle bar
16 125mm × 63mm × 7.5mm angle bar
17 Hull plates

A5/10 Frame 35, section of inner longitudinal bulkhead (1/100 scale)
1 Upper deck
2 70mm × 70mm × 7mm angle bar
3 6mm longitudinal plate
4 2.5mm longitudinal plates
5 60mm × 40mm × 5mm angle bar
6 4mm longitudinal plate
7 45mm × 45mm × 5mm angle bar
8 Lower deck
9 140mm × 60mm × 7mm × 10mm 'C' bar
10 5mm longitudinal plate
11 80mm × 60mm × 6mm angle bar
12 50mm × 50mm × 5mm angle bar
13 Platform deck
14 85mm × 85mm × 9mm vertical angle bar
15 120mm × 65mm × 7mm × 9mm 'C' bar

A5/11 Section at frame 124 (no scale)
1 Upper deck
2 Lower deck 20mm armour plates
3 Platform deck 5mm plates
4 Hold 6mm plates
5 Outer bottom 10–7mm plates
6 70mm × 70mm × 6mm angle bar
7 2.5mm longitudinal plates
8 60mm × 40mm × 5mm angle bar
9 50mm × 50mm × 5mm angle bar
10 4mm longitudinal plate
11 140mm × 60mm × 7mm × 10mm 'C' bar
12 85mm × 85mm × 9mm angle bar
13 120mm × 65mm × 9mm 'C' bar
16 18mm armour longitudinal plates
17 80mm × 60mm × 6mm angle bar
18 Hold
19 75mm × 60mm × 7mm angle bar
20 70mm × 70mm × 8mm angle bar
21 7mm bracket
22 160mm × 65mm × 7.5mm × 10mm 'C' bar
23 Hull plates

A5/12 Frame 160, section of inner longitudinal bulkhead (1/100 scale)
1 Lower deck
2 85mm × 85mm × 9mm angle bar
3 140mm × 60mm × 7mm × 10mm 'C' bar
4 18mm longitudinal armour plate
5 120mm × 65mm × 7mm × 9mm 'C' bar
6 70mm × 50mm × 7mm angle bar
7 Platform deck
8 95mm × 60mm × 7mm angle bar
9 Hold
10 64mm × 51mm × 7mm angle bar
11 50mm × 50mm × 7mm angle bar
12 64mm × 51mm × 7mm angle bar
13 160mm × 65mm × 7.5mm × 10.5mm 'C' bar
14 7mm bracket
15 5mm plate
16 Hull plates
14 70mm × 50mm × 6mm angle bar
15 15mm × 21mm × 3mm angle bar
16 70mm × 50mm × 6mm angle bar
17 5mm longitudinal plates
18 18mm armour longitudinal plates
19 95mm × 60mm × 7mm angle bar
20 60mm × 60mm × 7mm angle bar
21 50mm × 50mm × 6mm angle bar
22 75mm × 75mm × 9mm angle bar
23 70mm × 60mm × 7mm angle bar
24 90mm × 75mm × 10mm angle bar
25 80mm × 60mm × 6mm angle bar
26 80mm × 45mm × 6mm × 8mm 'C' bar
27 Inner bottom 7–6.5mm plates
28 50mm × 50mm × 6mm angle bar
29 64mm × 51mm × 7mm angle bar
30 5mm plate
31 6mm plate
32 125mm × 63mm × 6.5mm angle bar
33 6mm plate

A5/13 Double bottom, typical section (no scale)
1 Outer bottom 10mm plate
2 Inner bottom 7mm plate
3 6mm longitudinal plate

A5/14 Bilge keel structure (1/20 scale)
1 Hull plates
2 16mm rivets
3 12mm rivets
4 Flange
5 70mm × 70mm × 8mm angle bar
6 12.7mm rivets
7 70mm × 70mm × 7mm angle bar
8 6mm plates
9 8mm plate
10 16mm rivets in contact
11 60mm × 18mm bar riveted with 16mm rivets

4 7mm frame
5 12.7mm rivets
6 12.7mm rivets on flange
7 70mm × 70mm × 8mm angle bar
8 60mm × 60mm × 7mm angle bar
9 12.7mm rivets on angle bar
10 16mm rivets on angle bar

A5/15 Method of working lower deck armour with inner longitudinal bulkhead at frame 55 (no scale)
1 4mm longitudinal plates
2 2.5mm longitudinal plates
3 20mm lower deck armour plate
4 160mm × 60mm × 7mm × 100mm 'C' bar
5 50mm × 50mm × 5mm angle bar
6 70mm × 50mm × 6mm angle bar
7 60mm × 40mm × 5mm angle bar
8 9.5mm rivets
9 12.7mm rivets on angle bar
10 9mm rivets on angle bar

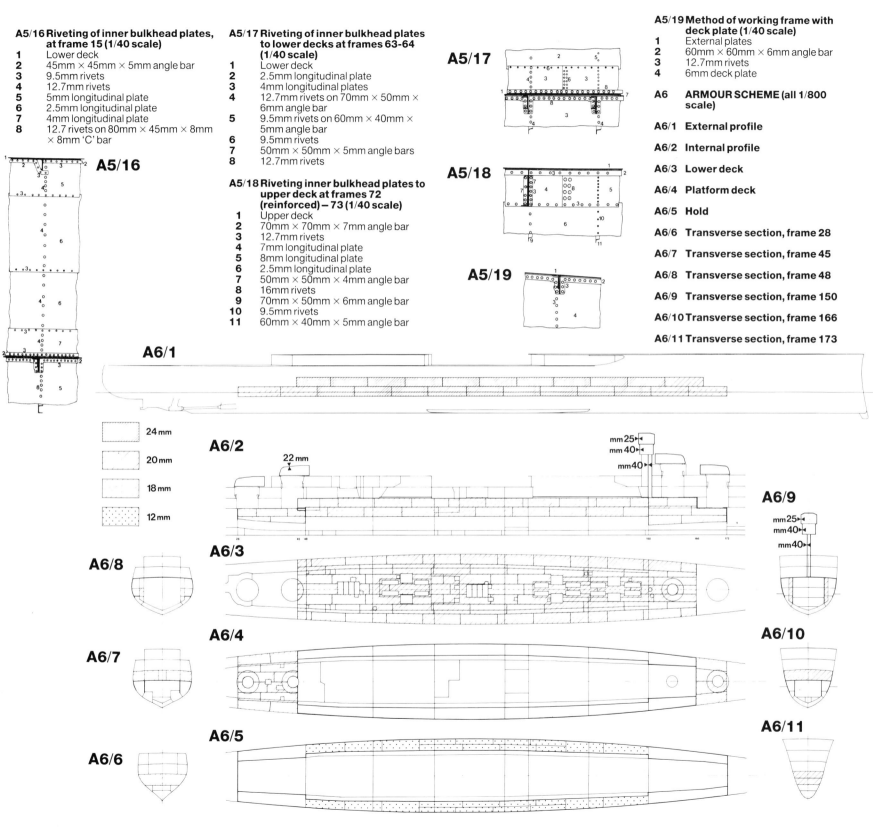

A5/16 Riveting of inner bulkhead plates, at frame 15 (1/40 scale)
1. Lower deck
2. 45mm × 45mm × 5mm angle bar
3. 9.5mm rivets
4. 12.7mm rivets
5. 5mm longitudinal plate
6. 2.5mm longitudinal plate
7. 4mm longitudinal plate
8. 12.7 rivets on 80mm × 45mm × 8mm × 8mm 'C' bar

A5/17 Riveting of inner bulkhead plates to lower decks at frames 63-64 (1/40 scale)
1. Lower deck
2. 2.5mm longitudinal plate
3. 4mm longitudinal plates
4. 12.7mm rivets on 70mm × 50mm × 6mm angle bar
5. 9.5mm rivets on 60mm × 40mm × 5mm angle bar
6. 9.5mm rivets
7. 50mm × 50mm × 5mm angle bars
8. 12.7mm rivets

A5/18 Riveting inner bulkhead plates to upper deck at frames 72 (reinforced) – 73 (1/40 scale)
1. Upper deck
2. 70mm × 70mm × 7mm angle bar
3. 12.7mm rivets
4. 7mm longitudinal plate
5. 8mm longitudinal plate
6. 2.5mm longitudinal plate
7. 50mm × 50mm × 4mm angle bar
8. 16mm rivets
9. 70mm × 50mm × 6mm angle bar
10. 9.5mm rivets
11. 60mm × 40mm × 5mm angle bar

A5/19 Method of working frame with deck plate (1/40 scale)
1. External plates
2. 60mm × 60mm × 6mm angle bar
3. 12.7mm rivets
4. 6mm deck plate

A6 ARMOUR SCHEME (all 1/800 scale)

A6/1 External profile

A6/2 Internal profile

A6/3 Lower deck

A6/4 Platform deck

A6/5 Hold

A6/6 Transverse section, frame 28

A6/7 Transverse section, frame 45

A6/8 Transverse section, frame 48

A6/9 Transverse section, frame 150

A6/10 Transverse section, frame 166

A6/11 Transverse section, frame 173

A5/16

A5/17

A5/18

A5/19

A6/1

24 mm
20 mm
18 mm
12 mm

A6/2

22 mm
mm 25
mm 40
mm 40

A6/3

A6/4

A6/5

A6/8

A6/7

A6/6

A6/9

mm 25
mm 40
mm 40

A6/10

A6/11

A General arrangements

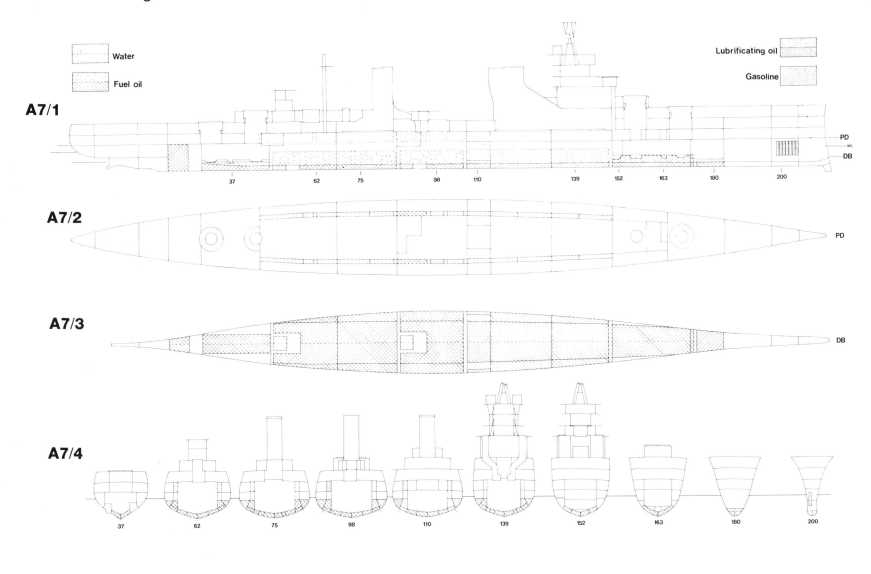

Water
Fuel oil
Lubrificating oil
Gasoline

A7/1

PD
wl.
DB

37 62 75 98 110 139 152 163 180 200

A7/2

PD

A7/3

DB

A7/4

37 62 75 98 110 139 152 163 180 200

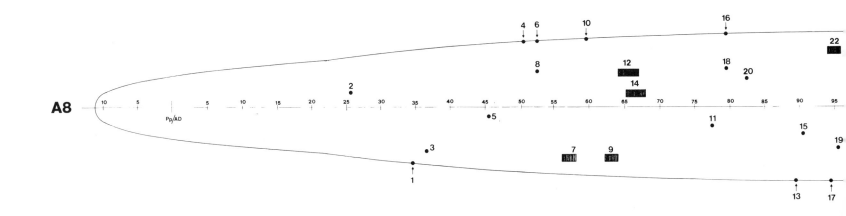

A8

A8   HULL VENTS AND OPENINGS (numbers are actual identification numbers; 1/400 scale)

1 Refrigeration water circulation discharge
2 50 tons per hour pump kingston valve
3 Refrigeration water circulation inlet
4 Bilge pump discharge
5 After powder magazine flooding kingston valve
6 Auxiliary condenser water circulation inlet (after engine)
7 Main condenser discharge (after engine)
8 Auxiliary condenser water circulation kingston valve (after engine)
9 Main condenser discharge (after engine)
10 Oil cooling water circulation discharge
11 Boiler drain discharge (boilers 5 and 6)
12 Main condenser water inlet (after engine)
13 Distillation circulation water discharge
14 Main condenser water inlet (after engine)
15 Evaporator discharge
16 Distillation circulation water discharge (boilers 5 and 6)
17 Auxiliary condenser water circulation inlet (forward engine)
18 Evaporator and distillation water inlet kingston valve
19 Auxiliary condenser water circulation kingston valve (forward engine)
20 Evaporator discharge (boilers 5 and 6)
21 Main condensor water inlet (forward engine)
22 Main condenser discharge (forward engine)
23 Oil cooling water circulation discharge
24 Main condenser discharge (forward engine)
25 Bilge pump discharge
26 Boiler drain discharge (boilers 3 and 4)
27 Main condenser water inlet (forward engine)
28 Boiler drain discharge (boilers 1 and 2)
29 Central magazine flooding kingston valve
30 150 tons per hour pump kingston valve
31 Refrigeration water circulation discharge
32 'Spada' submarine communications equipment
33 Refrigeration water circulation inlet
35 'Longevin' echo-sounder
37 Forward magazine flooding kingston valve
39 Refrigeration water circulation discharge
41 Refrigeration water circulation inlet
43 'Spalazzi' log

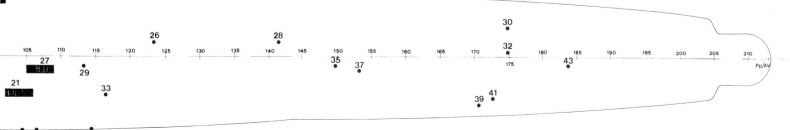

A General arrangements

A9/1

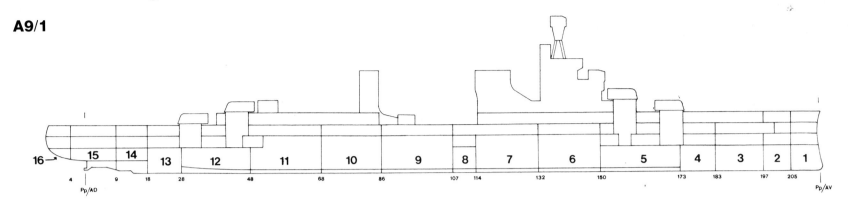

A9/2

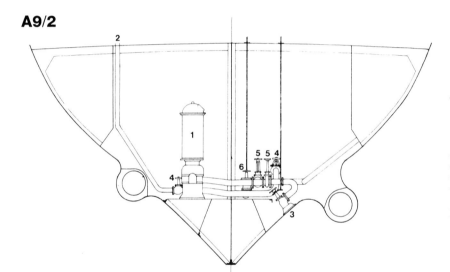

A9 PUMPING AND FLOODING ARRANGEMENTS

A9/1 Trials of stability in damaged state (ship at full load, 70009t, La Spezia, February 1931; no scale)

Trial	Flooded compart-ments	Draught forward (m)	Draught aft (m)	Mean draught (m)	Differ-ence (m)	Weight of water on board (t)
I	1,2,3,4	4.67	6.80	5.73	−2.13	585
II	4,5	4.59	7.35	5.97	−2.76	1052
III	5,6	4.60	8.08	6.34	−3.48	1880
IV	6,7	5.20	7.10	6.15	−1.90	1800
V	7,8,9	5.95	6.82	6.40	−0.85	2505
VI	10,9	6.50	5.75	6.12	+0.75	2068
VII	10,11	6.97	5.05	6.01	+1.92	1917
VIII	11,12	7.61	4.41	6.01	+3.20	1833
IX	13,12	7.21	4.28	5.74	+3.03	1090
X	13,14, 15,16	6.45	4.55	5.49	+1.90	421

A9/3

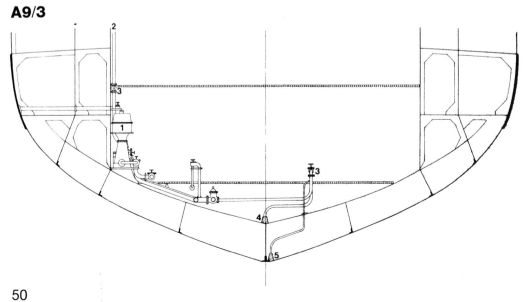

A9/4

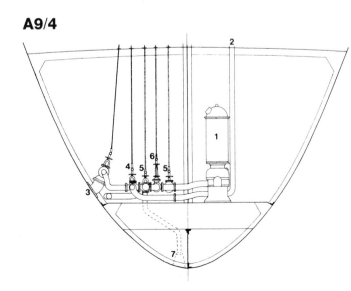

A9/2 150 tons per hour electric pump (frame 25 looking forward; 1/100 scale)

1 Electric driven pump
2 Delivery to fire main
3 Kingston intake and outboard discharge valve
4 Shut-off valve
5 Sluice valve
6 Non-return valve

A9/3 50 tons per hour electric pump (frame 55 looking forward; 1/100 scale)

1 Electric driven pump
2 Delivery to fire main
3 Shut-off valve
4 Bilge intake
5 Outer hull intake

A9/4 150 tons per hour electric pump (frame 175 looking aft; 1/100 scale)

1 Electric driven pump
2 To magazine
3 Intake and outboard discharge valve
4 Shut-off valve
5 Non-return valve
6 Sluice valve
7 Bilge intake

A9/5 Forward magazine flooding system, longitudinal section (1/50 scale)

A9/6 Transverse section, frame 152 looking forward

A9/7 Lower deck plan

1 Lower deck
2 Platform deck
3 Hold
4 Operating socket
5 Transmission rod
6 Stuffing box
7 Expansion joint
8 Bracket
9 Universal joint
10 Grating
11 150mm pipe for torpedo warhead store flooding
12 300mm pipe for magazine flooding
13 540mm seawater inlet

A9/8 Identification plate (1/2 scale)

A9/8

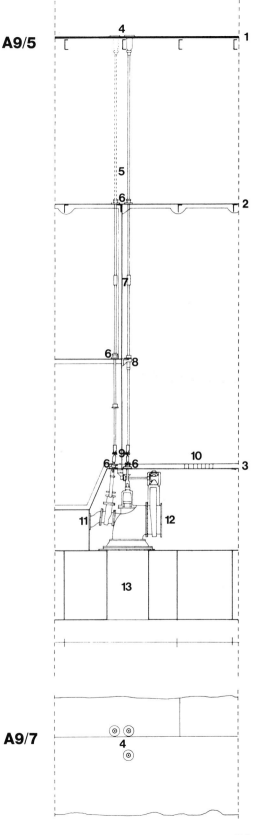

A General arrangements

A10/1

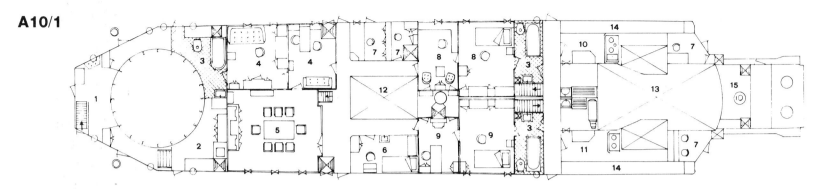

A10 **ACCOMMODATION (all 1/200 scale)**

A10/1 After superstructure
1 Guardhouse
2 Pantry
3 Bathrooms
4 Admiral's cabins
5 Briefing room
6 Flag lieutenant's cabin
7 Secretarys' offices
8 Captain's cabins
9 Chief of staff's cabins
10 Officers' galley
11 Admiral's and captain's galley
12 Skylight to engine room
13 Boiler uptakes
14 Reserve torpedo stowage
15 Forge

A10/2

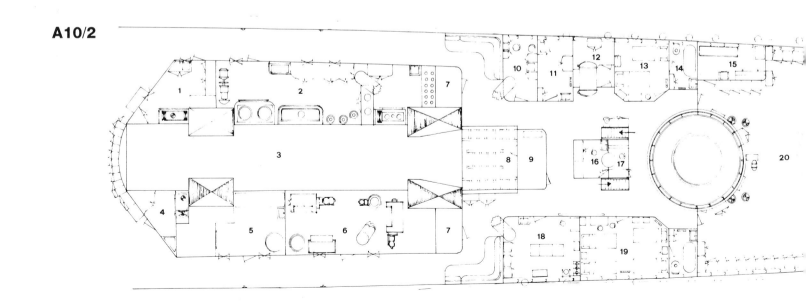

A10/3 Lower deck aft
1 Quartermaster's store
2 Officers' WC
3 Bathrooms
4 Officers' cabins
5 Executive officer's cabins
6 Wardroom
7 Cellar and pantry
8 Engineering officer's cabin
9 Paymaster's secretary's office
10 Paymaster's cabin
11 Supernumerary officer's cabin
12 Accountants' cabins

A10/3

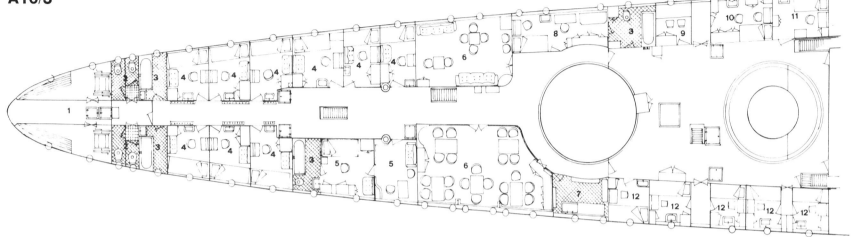

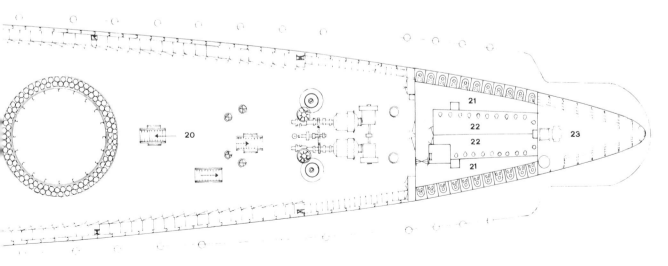

A10/2 Upper deck forward
1 Petty officers' galley
2 Crews' galley
3 Boiler uptakes
4 Hospital galley
5 Bakery
6 Laundry
7 Store
8 Linen store
9 Clothes pressing room
10 Barber
11 Sickbay attendant
12 Decontamination apparatus
13 Isolation ward
14 Isolation ward bathroom and WC
15 Secretary's office
16 Pharmacy
17 Mail office
18 First aid post
19 Crew hospital
20 Crew accommodation
21 Crew WCs
22 Crew urinals
23 Store

A General arrangements

A10/4 Lower deck forward
1 Crew wash places
2 Stokers' wash places and showers
3 Crews WCs
4 Petty officers' WC
5 Petty officers' washrooms and
showers
6 Boiler uptakes
7 Hatches to deck below
8 Crew urinals
9 Prison cell
10 Canteen
11 Refuelling pipes
12 Crew accommodation
13 Hammock stowage
14 Store

A10/4

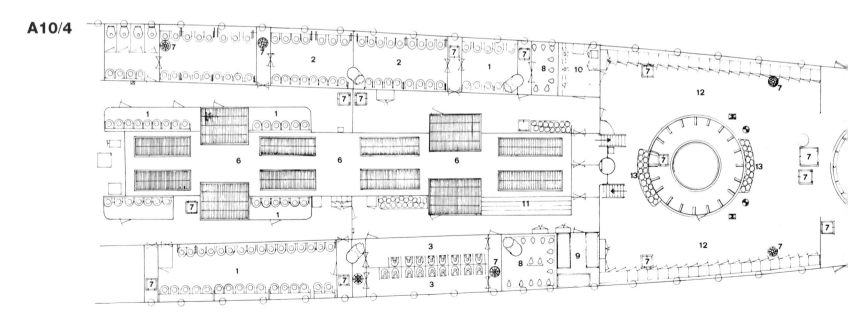

A10/5

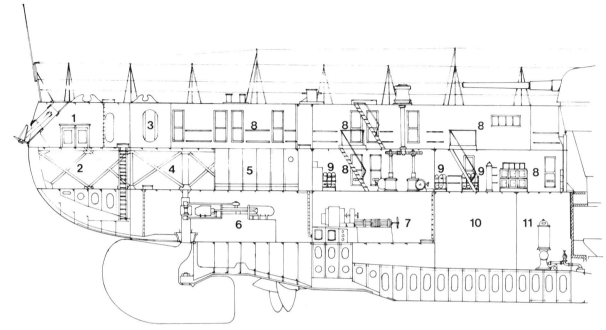

A10/5 Longitudinal section aft
1.   Store
2.   Quartermaster's store
3.   Officers' bath and WC
4.   Officers' baggage store
5.   Admiral's and captain's cellar and pantry
6.   Steering gear
7.   Steering gear machinery space
8.   Officers' cabins
9.   Officers' steward's hammock stowage
10. Fuel oil
11. Bilge pump

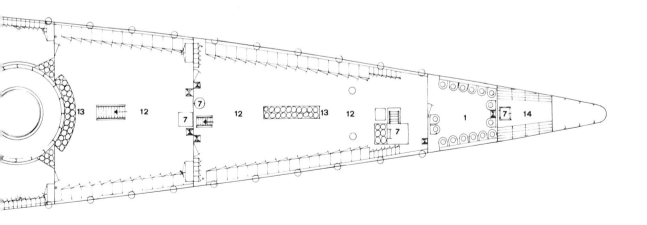

A General arrangements

A10/6 Longitudinal section forward
1 Crew accommodation
2 Crew WCs
3 Store
4 Crew wash place
5 Refrigeration machinery
6 Meat store
7 Pantry
8 Petty officers' baggage store
9 Bilge pump
10 Fuel for motor launches
11 Flour store
12 Wine store
13 Chain locker
14 Aviation fuel

A10/6

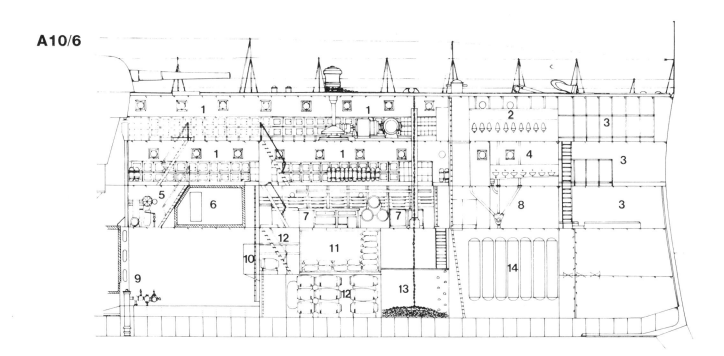

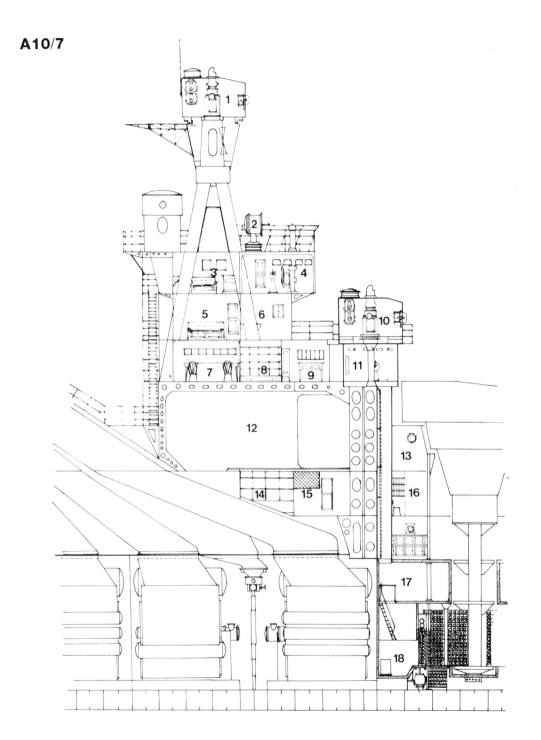

A10/7 Longitudinal section of bridge
1 Main director tower
2 90mm searchlight
3 Chartroom
4 Wheelhouse
5 Captain's sea cabin
6 Washroom and WC
7 Cipher office
8 Officers' library (from April 1939
  naval-air radio room)
9 Secretary's office
10 Armoured gun director
11 Conning tower
12 Hangar
13 Battery store
14 Linen store
15 Clothes pressing room
16 Main office
17 Transmitting station
18 Torpedo warhead magazine

A10/7

B1/1

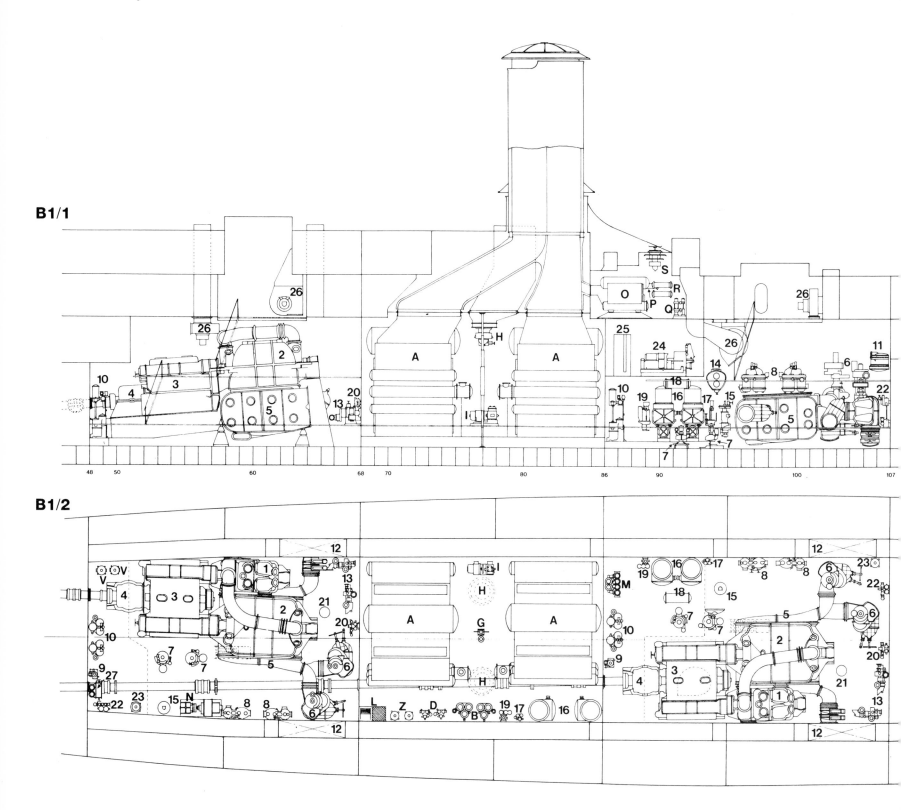

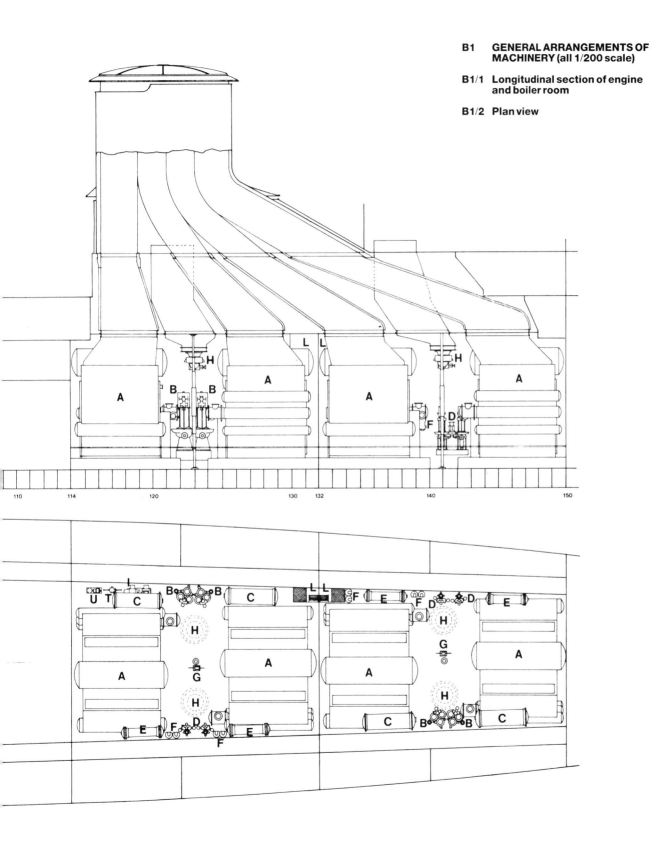

B1 GENERAL ARRANGEMENTS OF MACHINERY (all 1/200 scale)

B1/1 Longitudinal section of engine and boiler room

B1/2 Plan view

B Machinery

B1/3 Transverse section at frame 55
looking aft

B1/4 Transverse section at frame 64
looking aft

B1/5 Transverse section at frame 78
looking forward

B1/6 Transverse section at frame 92
looking aft

B1/3

B1/4

B1/5

B1/6

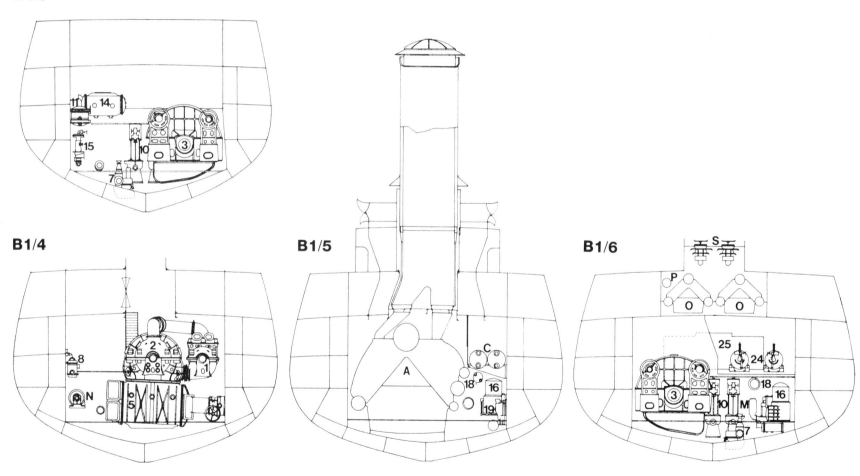

B1/8

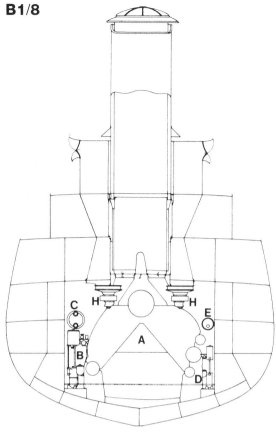

B1/7 Transverse section at frame 102 looking aft

B1/8 Transverse section at frame 123 looking forward

B1/9

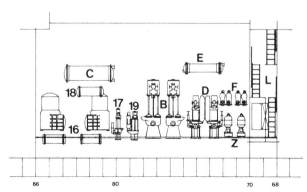

B1/7

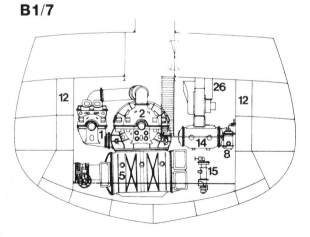

B1/10

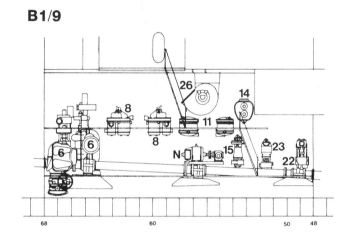

B1/9 Starboard side of after engine room

B1/10 Starboard side of after boiler room

Engines

1	High pressure turbine
2	Low pressure turbine
3	Gear case
4	Thrust block
5	Main condenser
6	Turbo-driven main condenser circulating pump
7	Turbo-driven main condenser extraction pump
8	Ejectors for main condenser
9	Lubricating oil purifier
10	Oil pump
11	Lubricating oil cooler
12	Feed water tank
13	Turbo driven main feed pump
14	Auxiliary condenser
15	Auxiliary condenser turbo-driven circulating and extraction pump
16	Evaporator
17	Evaporator pump
18	Distillater
19	Distillater pump
20	Cleaning drain pump
21	Observation cleaning drain tank
22	Steam driven bilge pump
23	Electric driven bilge pump
24	Turbo dynamo
25	Panel
26	Engine room ventilator
27	Oil filter

Boilers

A	Main boiler
B	Auxiliary feed pump
C	Feed water heater
D	Oil fuel feed pump
E	Oil fuel heater
F	Oil fuel filter set
G	First ignition hand driven pump
H	Boiler room ventilator
I	Air compressor
M	Steam driven refuelling pump
N	Electric driven refuelling pump
O	Auxiliary boiler
P	Auxiliary boiler water heater
Q	Fuel oil feed pump for auxiliary boiler
R	Oil fuel heater for auxiliary boiler
S	Auxililiary boiler room ventilator
T	Hand driven refuelling pump
U	Electric driven refuelling pump
V	Drinking water pump

B Machinery

B2 BOILERS

B2/1 External view of boiler framing
(1/50 scale)
1 Front
2 Side

B2/1

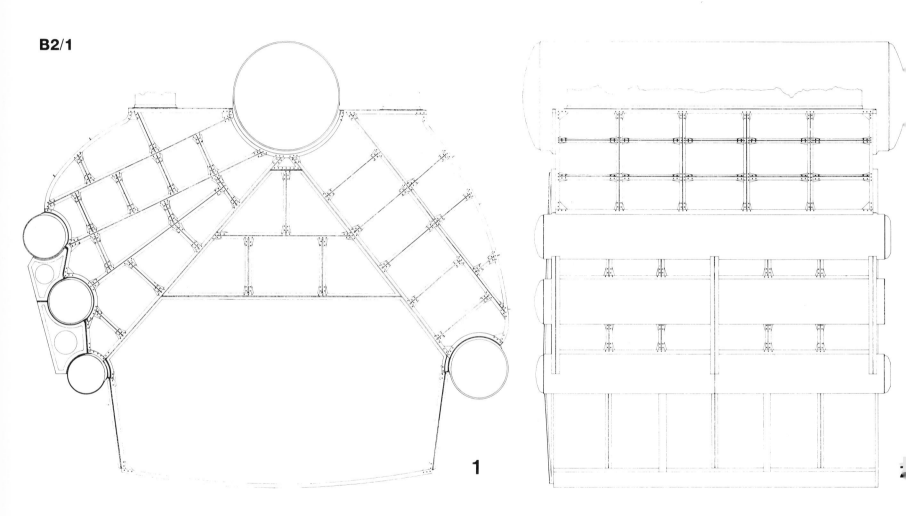

1

B2/2 Boiler frame details (1/25 scale; details 10 times scale)
1 2mm asbestos lagging
2 Fixing flange
3 12mm rivets
4 16mm bolts

B2/2

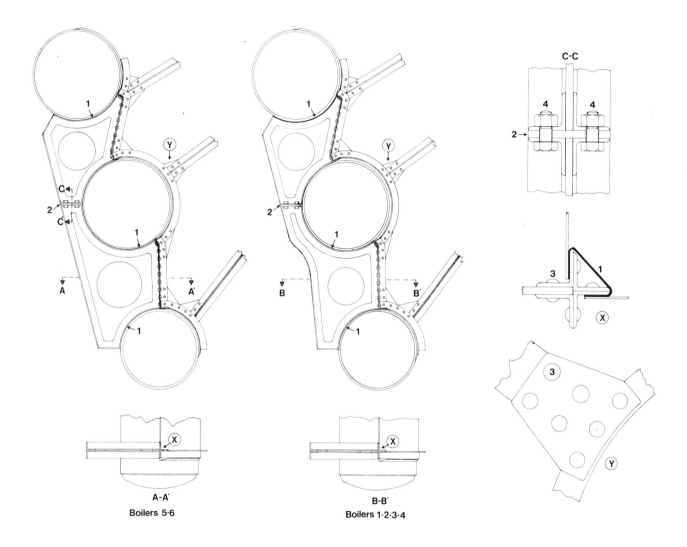

A-A'
Boilers 5·6

B-B'
Boilers 1·2·3·4

B Machinery

B2/3

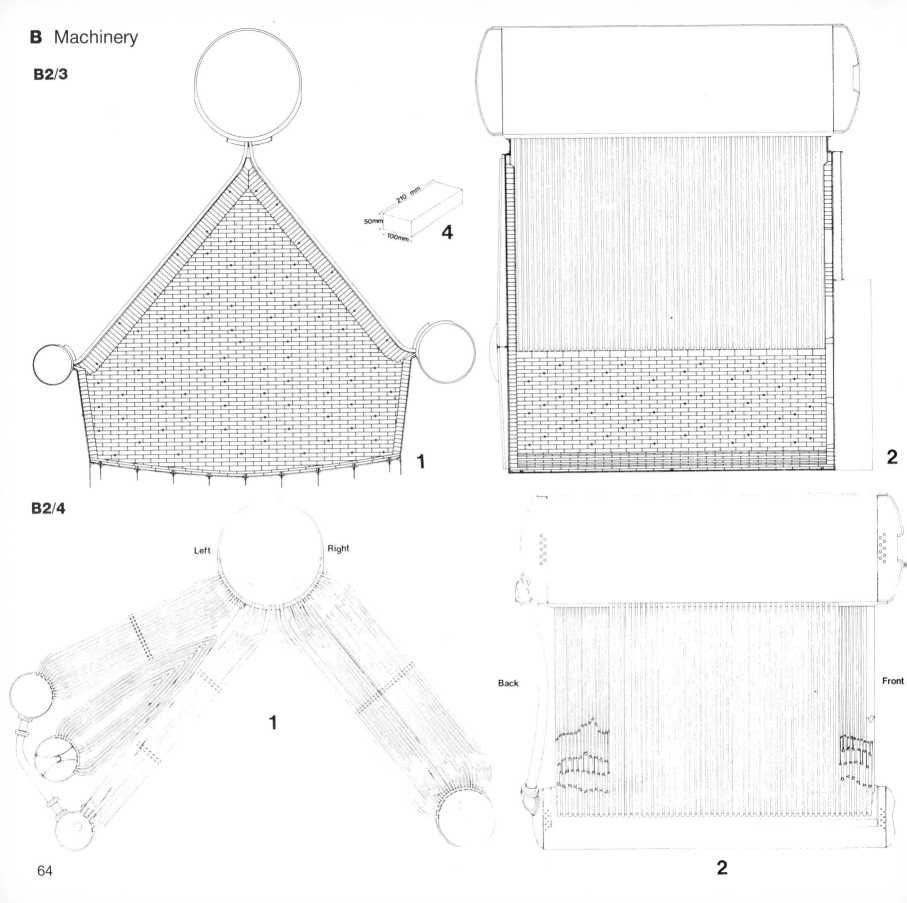

1

2

210 mm
50mm
100mm
4

B2/4

Left Right

1

Back Front

2

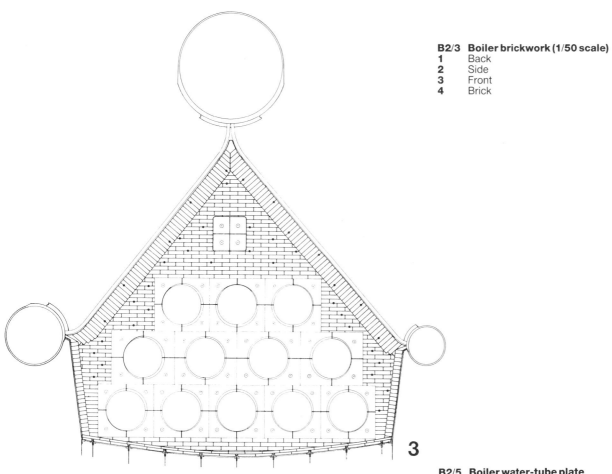

B2/3 Boiler brickwork (1/50 scale)
1 Back
2 Side
3 Front
4 Brick

3

B2/5 Boiler water-tube plate expansion (1/50 scale)
1 1919 tubes – 28.5mm outside diameter
2 176 tubes – 44.5mm outside diameter
3 309 tubes – 44.5mm outside diameter
4 1263 tubes – 28.5mm outside diameter

B2/4 Boiler water tubes (1/50 scale)
1 Front
2 Side

B2/5

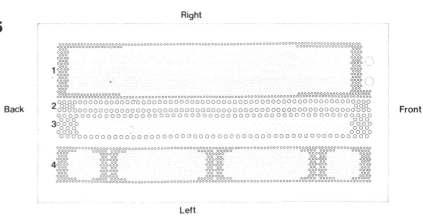

Right

Back

1
2
3

4

Front

Left

B Machinery

B2/6 Boiler fittings, front view (1/50 scale)

B2/7 Boiler fittings, elevation (1/50 scale)

1   Saturated steam stop valve for superheater
2   Saturated steam stop valve for auxiliary line
3   Saturated steam valve to superheater
4   Saturated steam valve to main line
5   Superheated main steam stop valve
6   Superheated auxiliary steam stop valve
7   Stop valves for water level indicators
8   Water level indicators
9   Double full bore safety valve
10 Auxiliary feed valve
11 Main feed valve
12 Automatic regulator feed steam stop valve
13 Automatic regulator feed water stop valve
14 Automatic regulator
15 Air course cock
16 Cock for superheated steam pressure gauge
17 Safety valve for superheater
18 Slide valve box for fuel oil to sprayers
19 Fuel oil thermometer
20 Superheated steam thermometer
21 Blow-off valve
22 Superheater flood valve
23 Superheater drain valve
24 Superheater flood and drain stop valve
25 Oil fuel sprayers
26 Oil fuel sprayer gauge
27 Smoke observation mirrors

B2/6

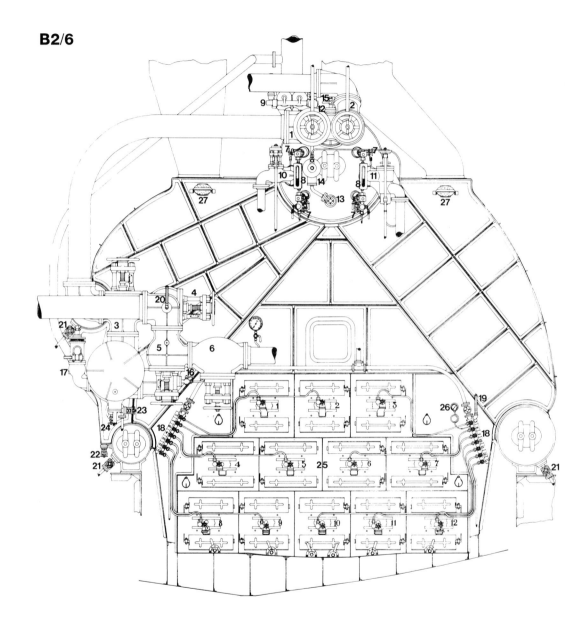

B2/7

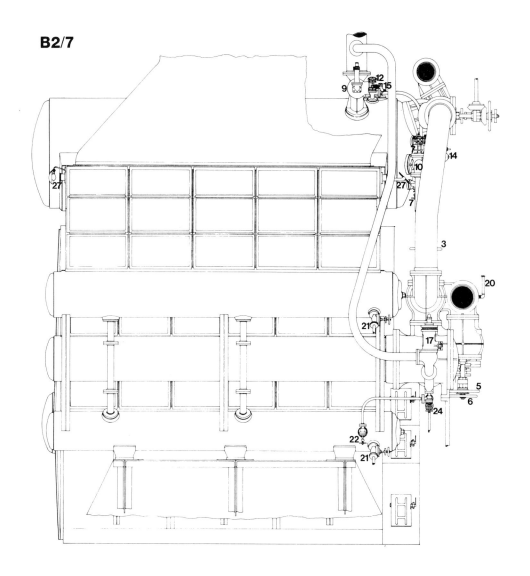

B Machinery

B2/8

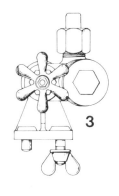

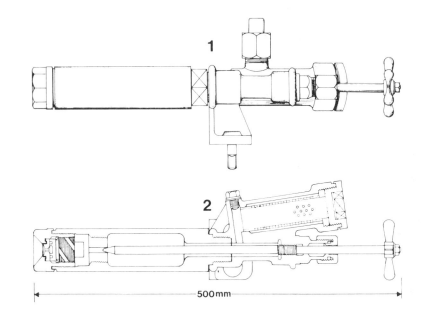

500mm

B2/8 Fuel oil sprayer (1/5 scale)
1 Profile
2 Section
3 Rear view

B2/9 Auxiliary boiler (1/50 scale)
1 Fuel oil sprayers
2 Down-flow tubes
3 Steam drums
4 Water drums
5 Combustion chamber
6 Water tubes

B2/10 Auxiliary boiler, water-tube plate expansion (1/50 scale)
1 409 tubes, 28.5mm outside diameter
2 130 tubes, 38mm outside diameter
3 410 tubes, 28.5mm outside diameter
4 4 downflow tubes, 75mm outside diameter

B2/10

B3/1

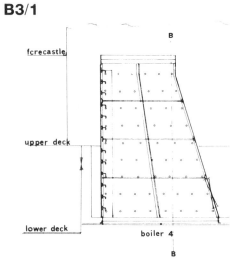

B2/9

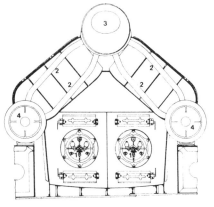

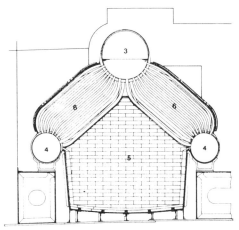

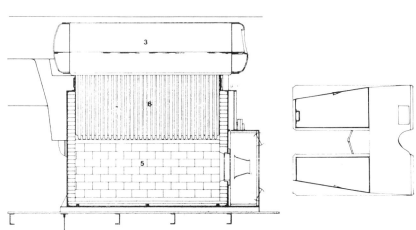

68

B3   FUNNELS (all 1/100 scale)

B3/1   Uptakes from boilers 1–4
1   Transverse section
2   Longitudinal section
3   Plan view

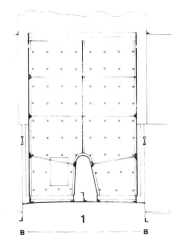

1

B — — — B

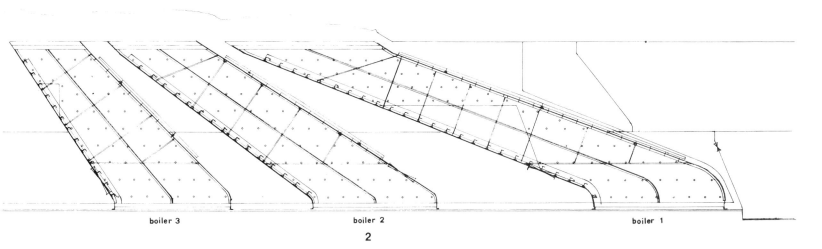

boiler 3   boiler 2   boiler 1

2

3

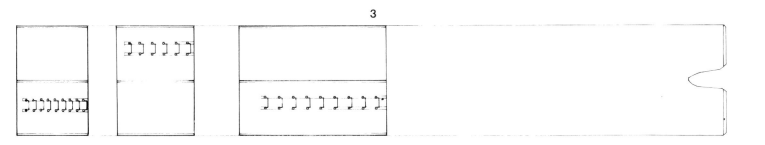

B Machinery

B3/2 Forward funnel
1 Longitudinal section
2 Plan view
3 Transverse section
4 Outline of uptakes

B3/2

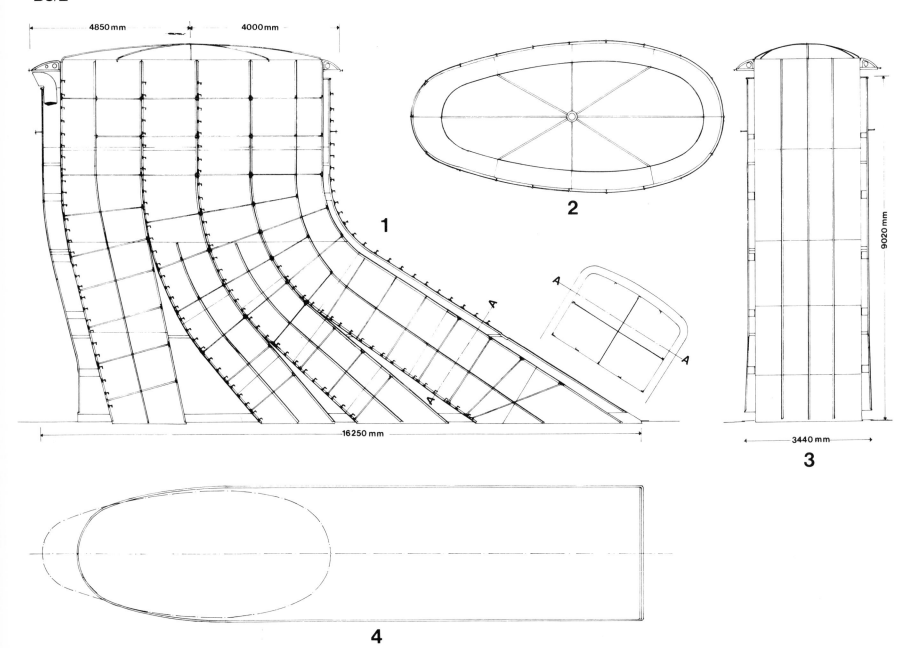

B3/3 Uptakes from boilers 5 and 6
1 Transverse section
2 Longitudinal section
3 Plan view

B3/3

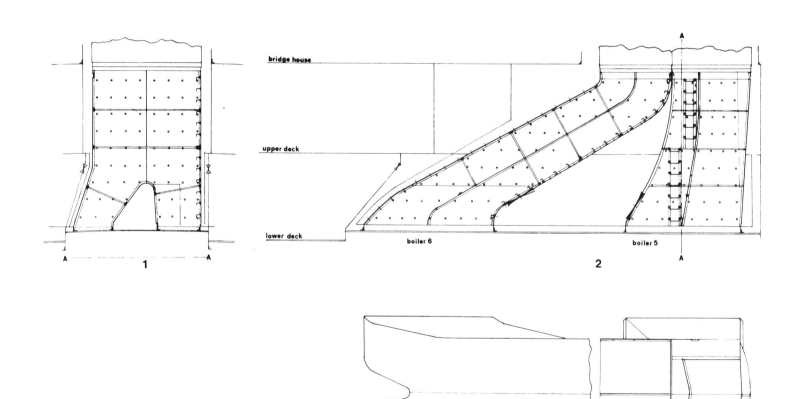

1

bridge house

upper deck

lower deck

boiler 6   boiler 5

2

3

B Machinery

B3/4 **After funnel**
1 Longitudinal section
2 Transverse section
3 Horizontal section at A–A
4 Horizontal section at B–B
5 Plan view

B3/4

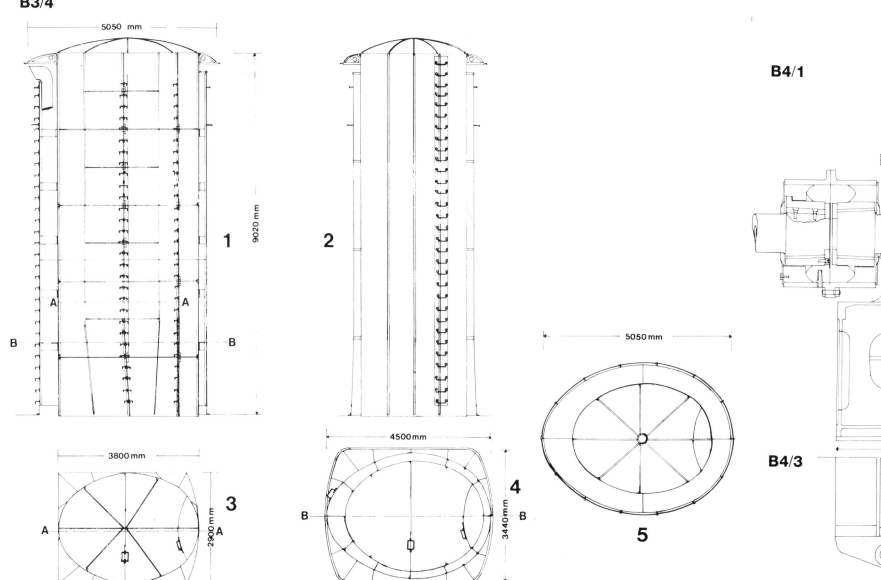

B4/1

B4/3

B4/1   **High pressure turbine, longitudinal section (1/25 scale)**
1   Main steam inlet
2   Exhaust steam to low pressure turbine
3   Thrust block

B4/2   **High pressure turbine, rear elevation (1/25 scale)**
1   Main steam inlet

B4/3   **High pressure turbine, half plan (1/25 scale)**
1   Main steam inlet
2   Exhaust steam to low pressure turbine
3   Full power
4   Half power
5   Reverse
6   Cruising speed
7   Auxiliary steam at cruising speed
8   Discharge valve

B4/2

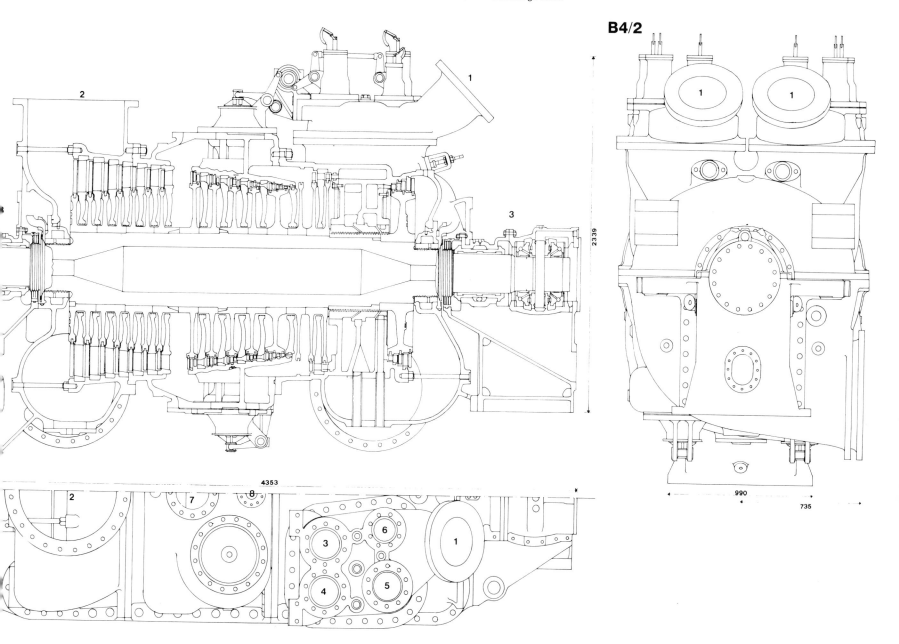

B Machinery

B4/4 Low pressure turbine (1/25 scale)
1 Auxiliary steam at full power
2 Main steam inlet
Thrust block

B4/5 Main condenser (1/50 scale)
1 Plan view
2 Left side
3 Right side
4 Front view
5 Transverse section

B4/4

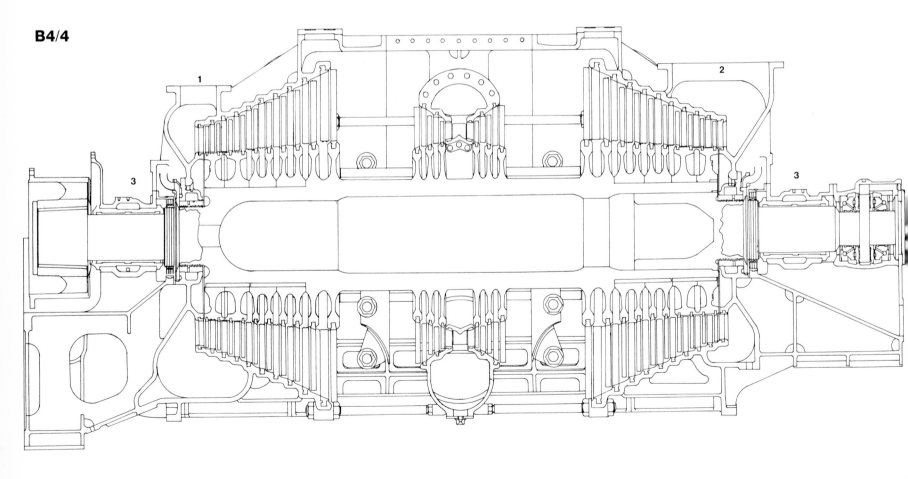

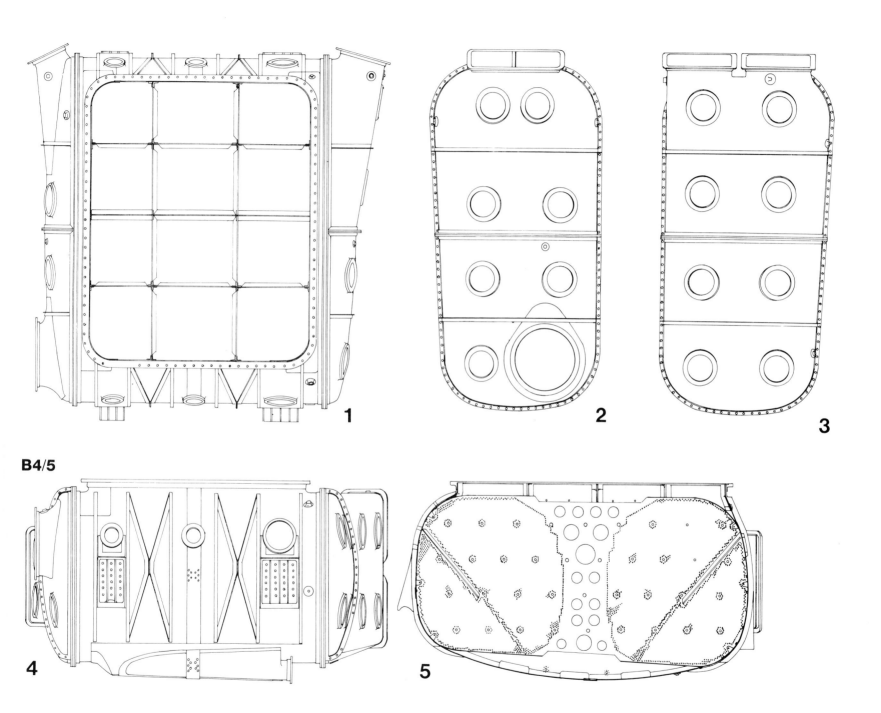

B4/5

1

2

3

4

5

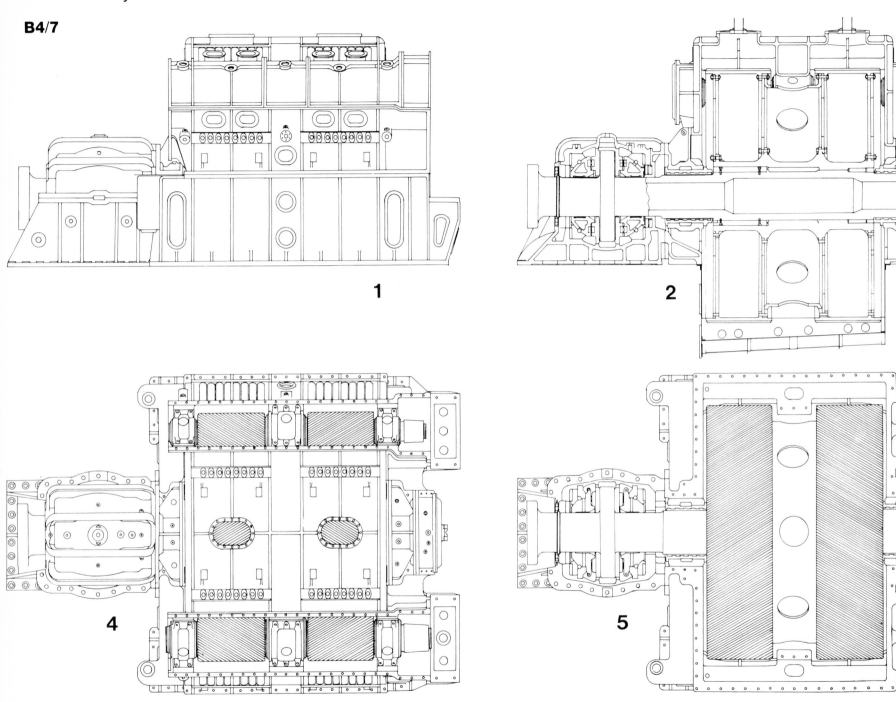

1

2

4

5

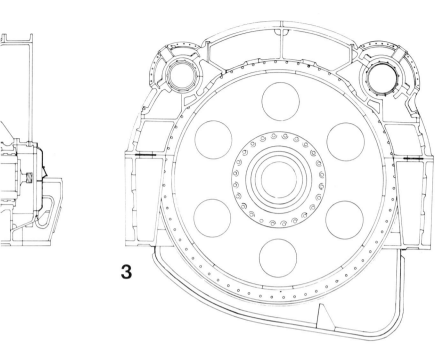

B4/6 Auxiliary condenser (1/50 scale)
1   Transverse section
2   Longitudinal section
3   Front elevation
4   Rear elevation
5   Plan (half) and section (half)

B4/7 Reduction gearing and thrust blocks (1/50 scale)
1   Gear case elevation
2   Longitudinal section
3   Front view
4   Plan view
5   Horizontal section of casing

3

B4/6

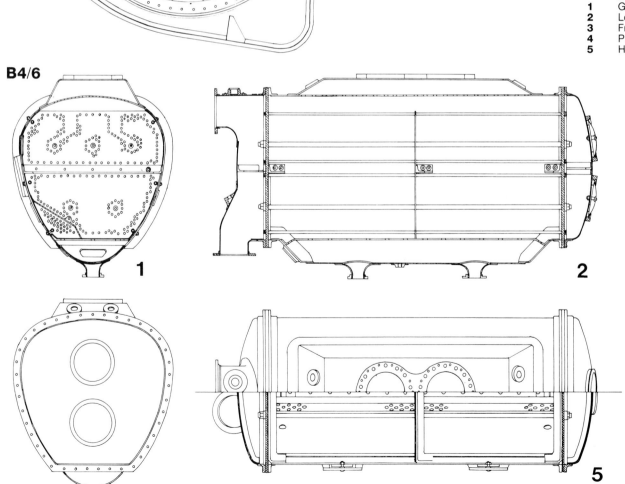

1

2

3

4

5

B Machinery

B5 **PROPELLER SHAFTS (all 1/100 scale)**

B5/1 **Port propeller shaft elevation (angled 73.33 per cent from horizontal)**

B5/2 **Starboard propeller shaft elevation (angled 40.66 per cent from horizontal)**

B5/3 **Plan view (port shaft angled 28.65 per cent from centreline; starboard 14.66 per cent)**

B5/4 **Transverse section at frame 36**

B5/5 **Transverse section on after perpendicular**
1 After engine room
2 After boiler room (boilers 5 and 6)
3 Forward engine room
4 Friction brake
5 Torsion meter

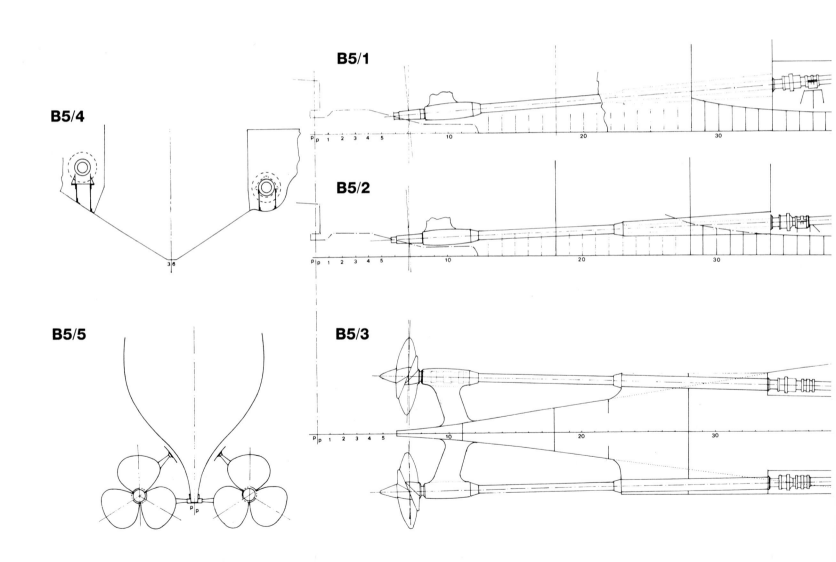

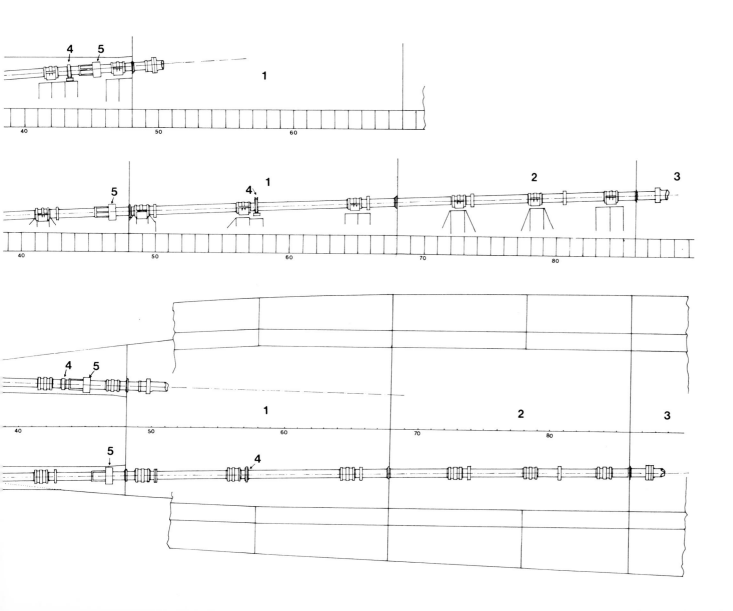

B Machinery

B5/6 Propeller (1/25 scale)
Diameter – 4.400m
Uniform Pitch – 4.88m
Projected surface area 11.11m^2
Developed surface area – 12.66m^2
Max power per shaft – 48,000shp
Max revolutions – 300
1 Starboard screw propeller looking aft
2 Sectioned elevation of propeller boss
3 Sections of the blade

B5/6

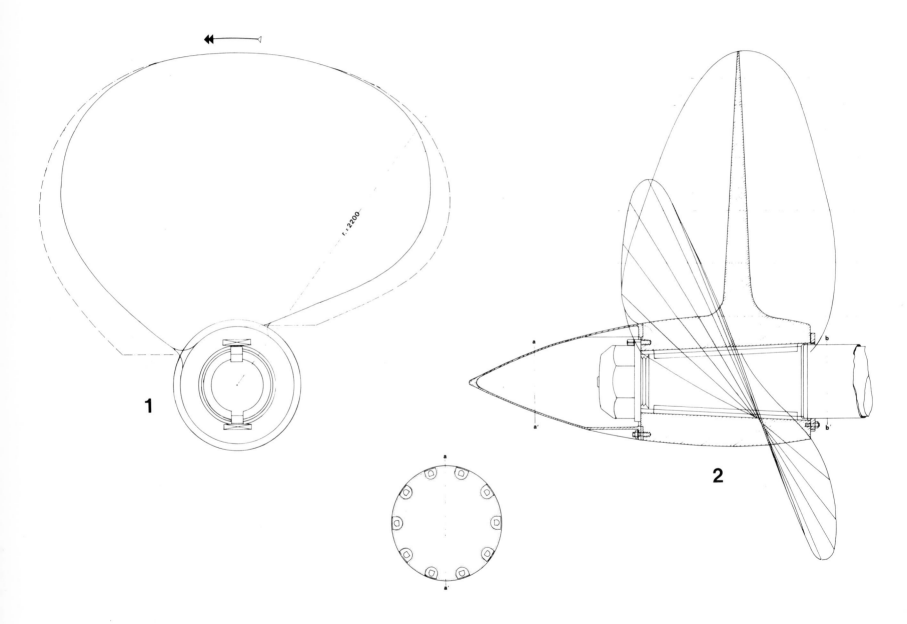

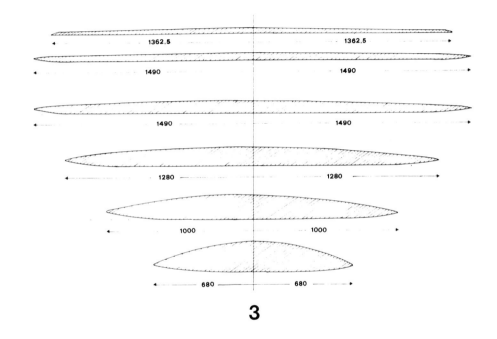

1362.5   1362.5

1490   1490

1490   1490

1280   1280

1000   1000

680   680

3

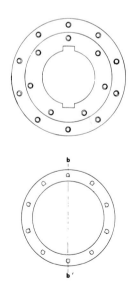

b

b'

B6/1

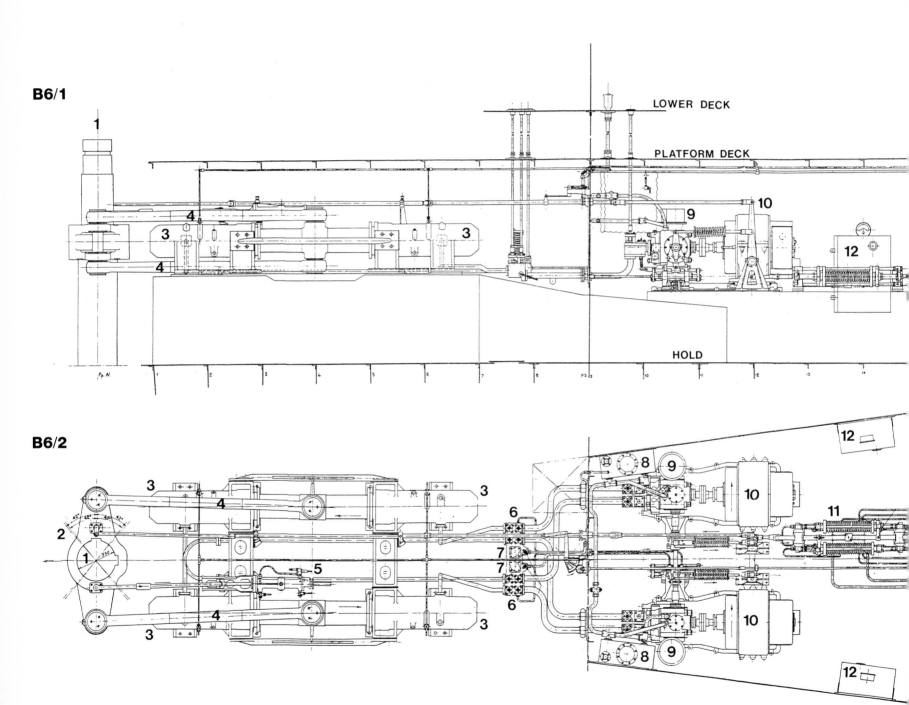

LOWER DECK

PLATFORM DECK

HOLD

B6/2

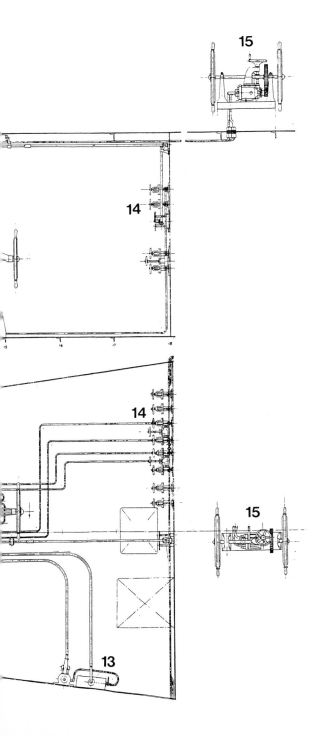

B6   STEERING MACHINERY

B6/1   Longitudinal section (1/50 scale)

B6/2   Plan view (1/50 scale)
 1   Rudder shaft
 2   Effective turning angles
 3   Cylinders
 4   Connecting rods
 5   Helm indicator transmitter cylinder
       (ball and triangle on the main mast)
 6   Shut-off valves
 7   Relief valves
 8   Main oil tank
 9   Solenoid
10   Electric motors
11   Receiver telemotor cylinders
12   Electric motor control panels
13   Charging oil tank
14   Valves
15   Rudder hand operation

B6/3   Telemotor for hydraulic rudder
           operation (1/25 scale)

B6/4   Transmitter section
 1   Oil tank
 2   Charging pump
 3   Telemotor receiver
 4   Charging valve
 5   Circulating valve
 6   Non-return valve
 7   Transmitter, longitudinal section
 8   Steering wheel
 9   Helm indicator
10   Toothed arc
11   Telemotor receiving cylinder
12   Piston
13   Automatic by-pass
14   Transmitter, transversel section
15   By-pass valve

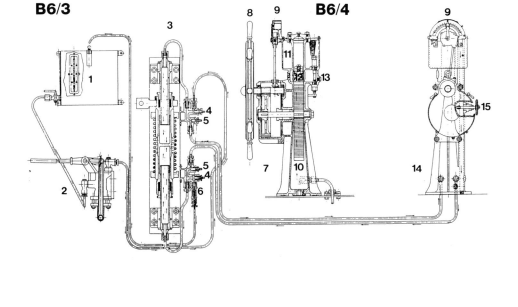

B6/3

B6/4

C Projected AA conversions

C1 LAYOUT OF FIRST PROPOSAL (COMITATO PROGETTI NAVI) TO CONVERT *DI GIUSSANO* CLASS CRUISERS TO ANTI–AIRCRAFT SHIPS (no scale)

C2 SECOND PROJECTED CONVERSION (ODERO–TERNI–ORLANDO, MUGGIANO–LA SPEZIA), MARCH 1938 (no scale)

C2/1 Sheer and plan view

C1

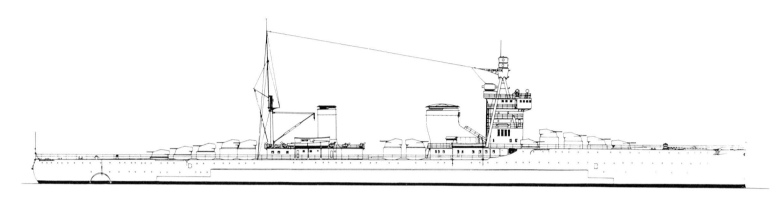

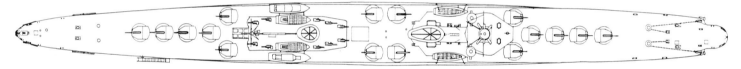

C2/1

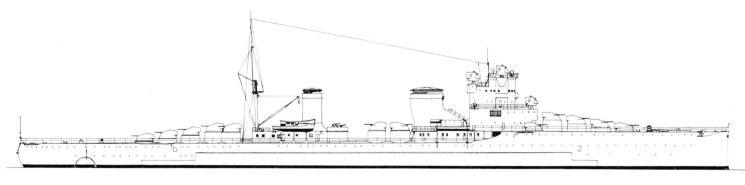

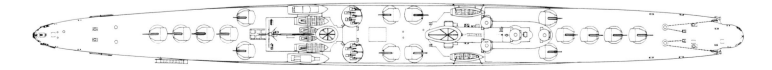

C2/2 Internal profile
1   After magazine
2   After engine room
3   After boiler room (boilers 5 and 6)
4   Forward engine room
5   Midships magazine
6   Central boiler room (boilers 3 and 4)
7   Forward boiler room (boilers 1 and 2)
8   Forward magazine

C2/2

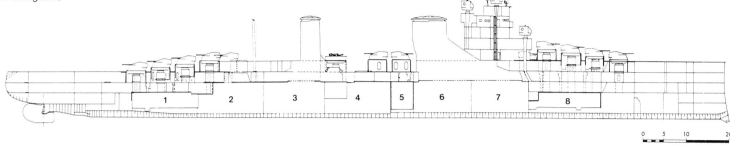

0   5   10   20
                       m

C3/1

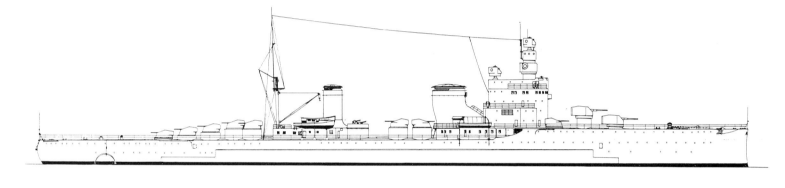

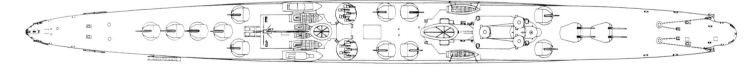

C3   THIRD PROJECTED CONVERSION (COMITATO PROGETTI NAVI/OTO, LA SPEZIA), JUNE 1938 (no scale)

C3/1   Original scheme

C3/2   Alternative arrangement of light AA guns

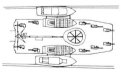

C3/2

D Ground tackle

D1/1

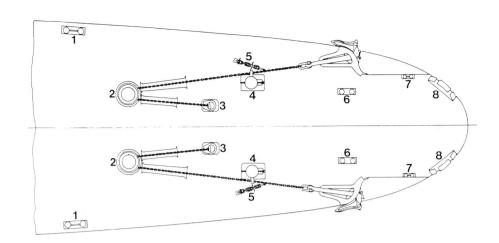

D1/2

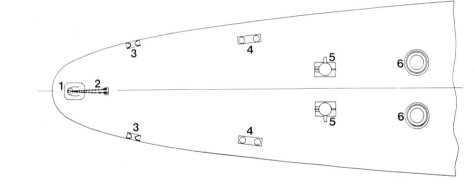

D2/1

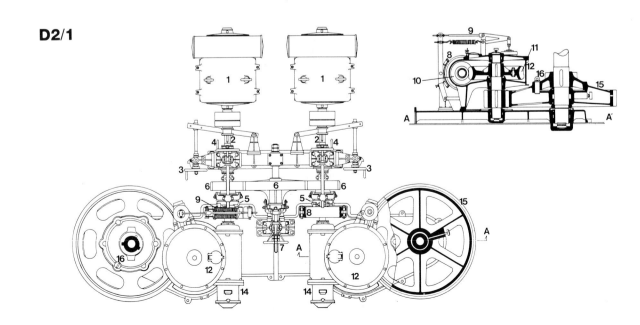

D2/2

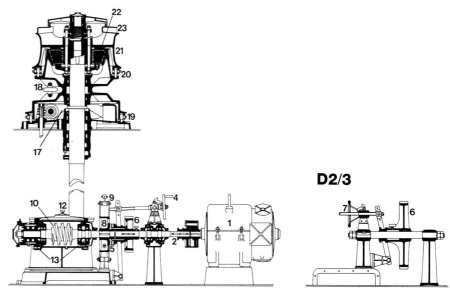

D2/3

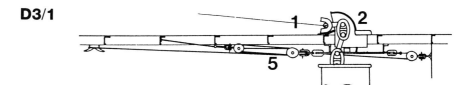

D3/1

D3/2

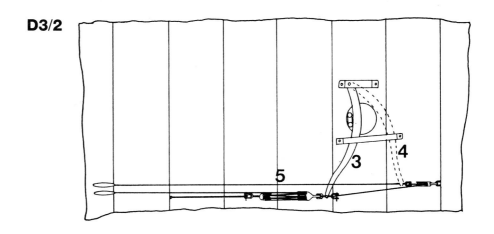

D Ground tackle

D4 **CHAIN STOPPER (1/50 scale)**
1   Turnbuckle
2   Pelican hook or slip

D5 **CHAIN CABLE**

D5/1 **Details of chain (1/50 scale)**
1   Outboard end
2   First length (25m, 121 links)
3   Following lengths (as above)
4   Last length (as above)
5   Shackle
6   Swivel
7   Reinforced link
8   Simple link
9   'Kenter' shackle
10   Last link to shackle in chain locker

D5/2 **'Kenter' shackle (1/10 scale)**
1   Plan
2   Lateral view
3   Plumb bolt

D6 **BOWER ANCHOR (4000kg; 1/50 scale)**

D4

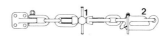

D6

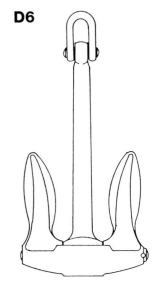

D5/2

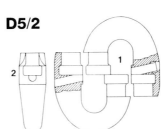

D5/1

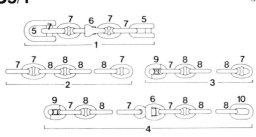

88

D8/1

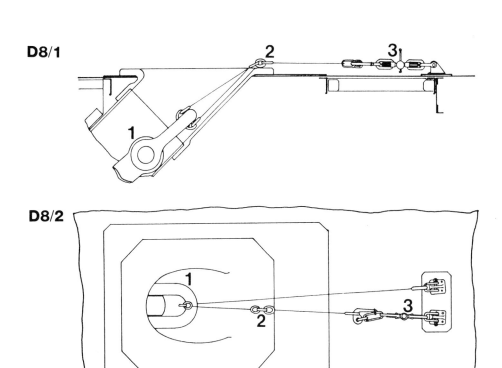

D7

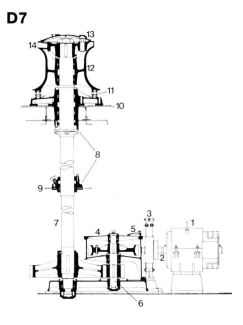

D8/2

D9

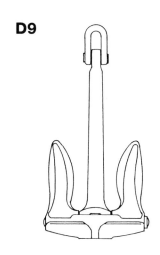

D7   AFTER WARPING CAPSTAN (1/50 scale)
1   26hp electric motor
2   Transmission axle
3   Brake
4   Case for gearing in oil bath
5   Oil filler cap
6   Transmission gear
7   Axle
8   Stuffing box
9   Lower deck
10   Upper deck
11   Capstan pawls
12   Warping drum
13   Retaining pin between drum and axle
14   Socket for capstan bars

D8   STOPPER FOR STERN (STREAM) ANCHOR (1/50 scale)

B1/1   Longitudinal section

D8/2   Plan view
1   Stream anchor
2   Breeching chain
3   Turnbuckle

D9   STREAM ANCHOR (2000kg; stowed in stern hawsepipe; 1/50 scale)

E Rig

E1 MAIN MAST (1/200 scale)

E1/1 Elevation

E1/2 Front view
1 Dressing line
2 White masthead light
3 Paired lights
4 Ensign halliard
5 Radio aerial
6 10-ton derrick
7 Rudder angle indicator
8 Top light (admiral's light)

E1/1

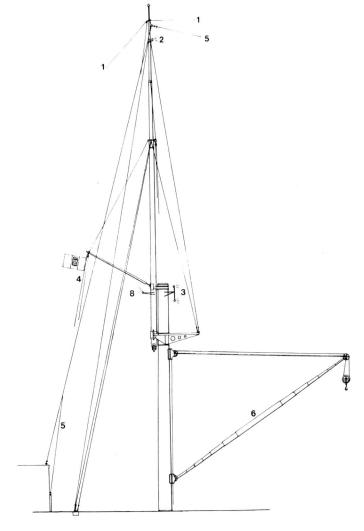

E1/2

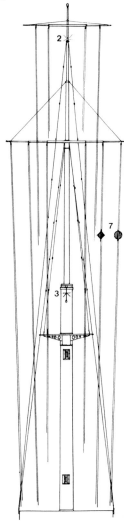

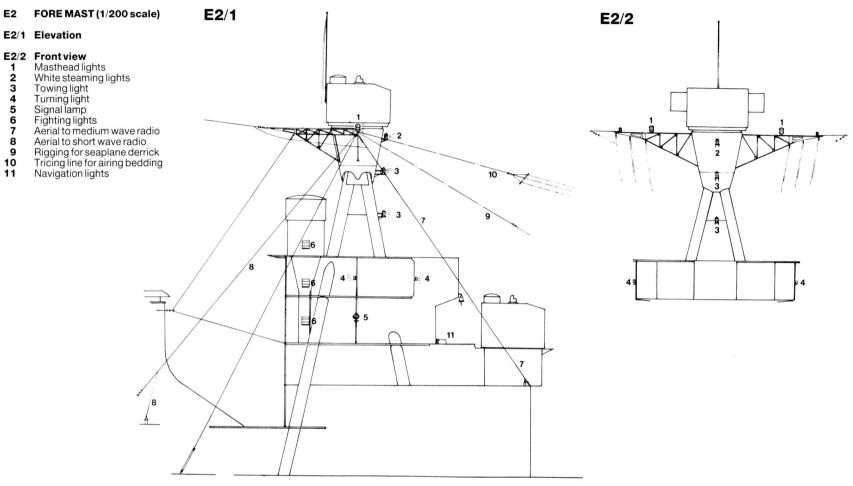

E2　FORE MAST (1/200 scale)

E2/1　Elevation

E2/2　Front view
1　Masthead lights
2　White steaming lights
3　Towing light
4　Turning light
5　Signal lamp
6　Fighting lights
7　Aerial to medium wave radio
8　Aerial to short wave radio
9　Rigging for seaplane derrick
10　Tricing line for airing bedding
11　Navigation lights

E2/1

E2/2

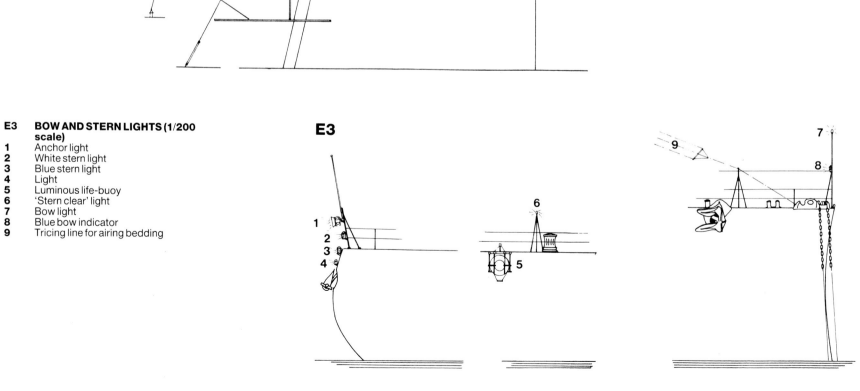

E3　BOW AND STERN LIGHTS (1/200 scale)
1　Anchor light
2　White stern light
3　Blue stern light
4　Light
5　Luminous life-buoy
6　'Stern clear' light
7　Bow light
8　Blue bow indicator
9　Tricing line for airing bedding

E3

E Rig

E4   DERRICK WINCH (1/25 scale)

E4/1   Longitudinal section

E4/2   Transverse section

E4/3   Plan view
1   First brake
2   Second brake
3   Handwheel for second brake
4   Shaft bearings
5   Worm and screw gearing
6   Spur gearing
7   Gear box
8   Flexible coupling
9   Electric motor
10   Barrel

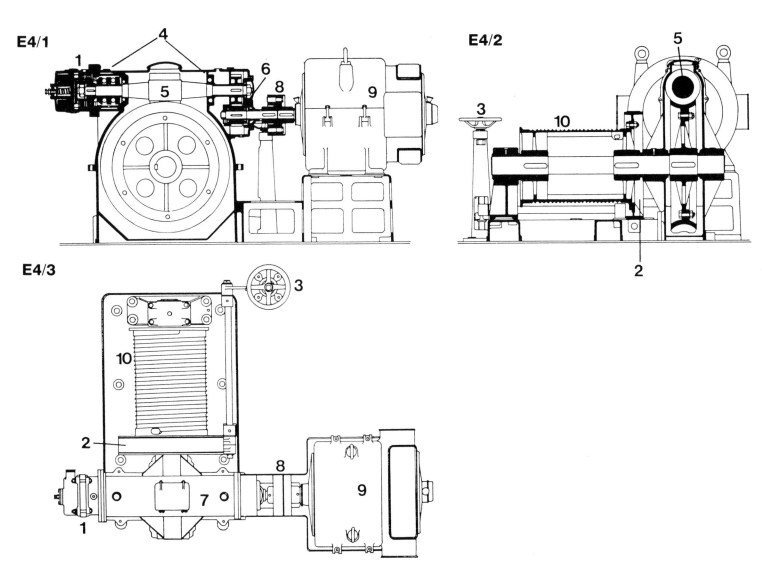

F Boats

F1

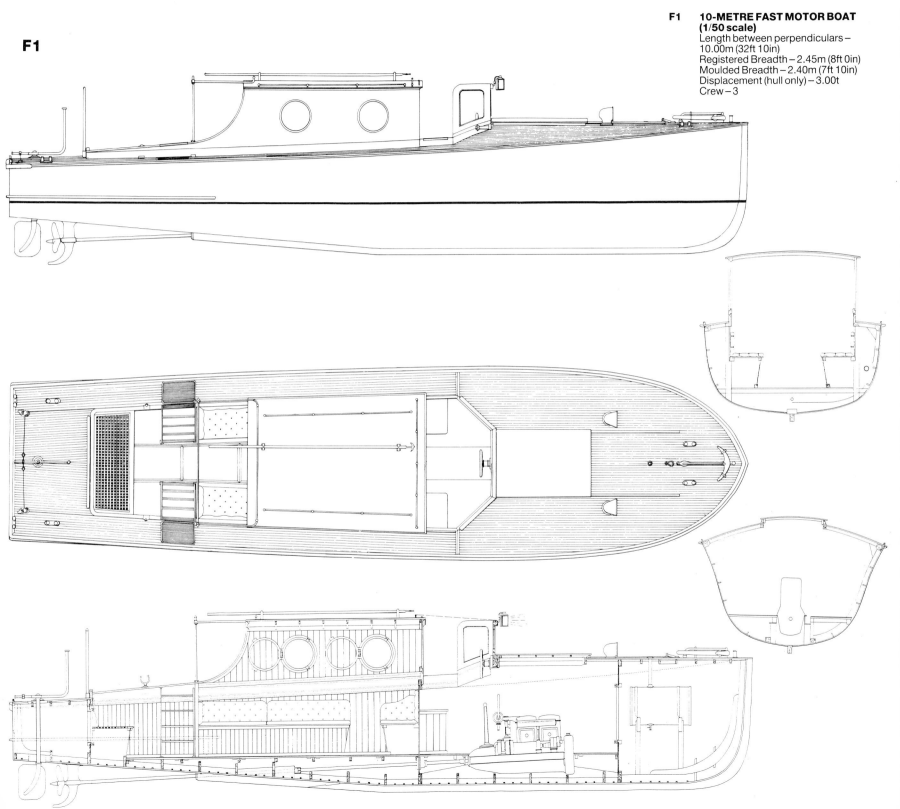

F1 **10-METRE FAST MOTOR BOAT
(1/50 scale)**
Length between perpendiculars –
10.00m (32ft 10in)
Registered Breadth – 2.45m (8ft 0in)
Moulded Breadth – 2.40m (7ft 10in)
Displacement (hull only) – 3.00t
Crew – 3

F Boats

F2

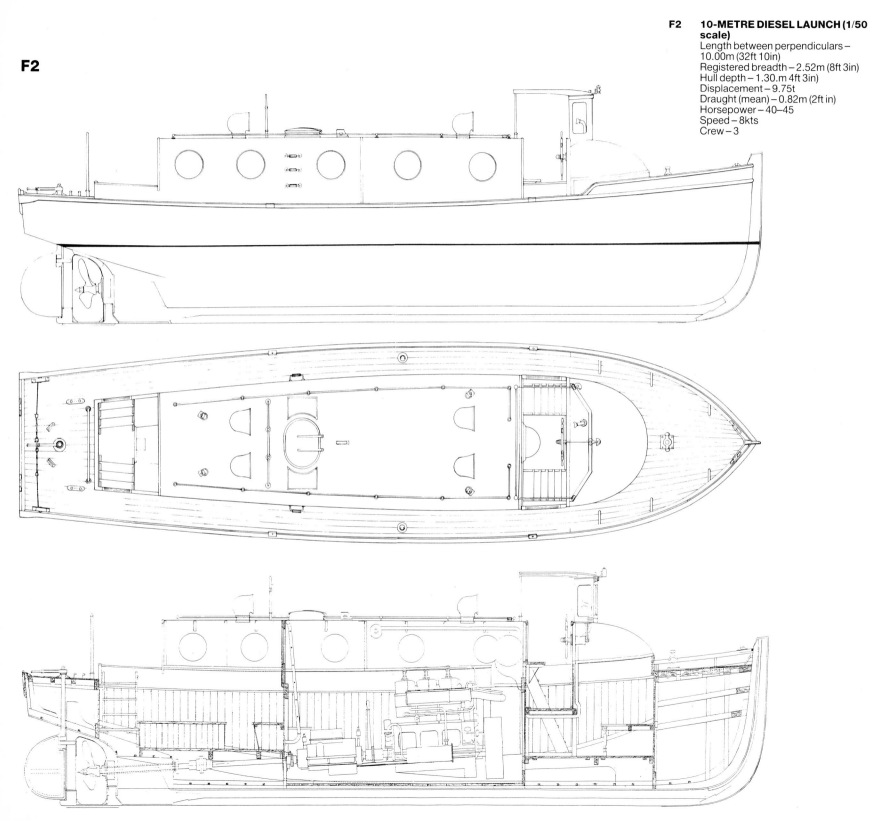

F2   10-METRE DIESEL LAUNCH (1/50 scale)
Length between perpendiculars –
10.00m (32ft 10in)
Registered breadth – 2.52m (8ft 3in)
Hull depth – 1.30.m 4ft 3in)
Displacement – 9.75t
Draught (mean) – 0.82m (2ft in)
Horsepower – 40–45
Speed – 8kts
Crew – 3

F3

F3   **8.6-METRE LAUNCH
(UNSINKABLE PULLING BOAT;
1/50 scale)**
Length between perpendiculars –
8.60m (28ft 3in)
Registered breadth – 2.40m (7ft 10in)
Moulded breadth – 2.36m (7ft 9in)
Hull depth – 0.88m (2ft 11in)
Weight (hull only) – 1500 kg (3300lbs)
Equipment weight – 150kg (330lbs)

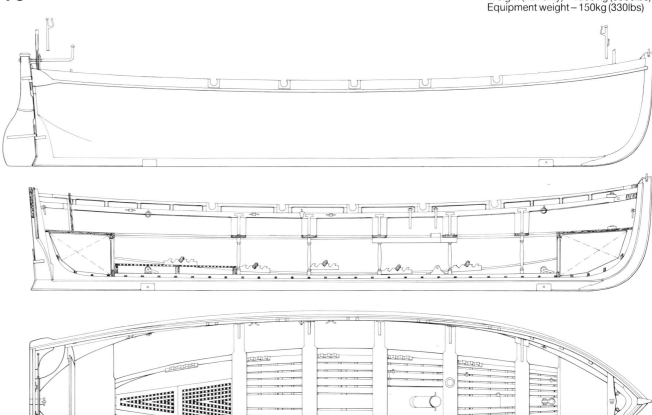

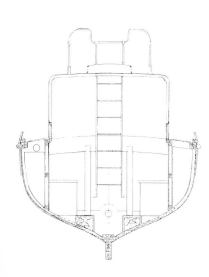

95

F Boats

F4 8.5-METRE 12-OARED GIG (1/50 scale)
Length between perpendiculars –
8.50m (27ft 11in)
Registered breadth – 2.00m (6ft 8in)
Depth – 0.86m (2ft 10in)

F4

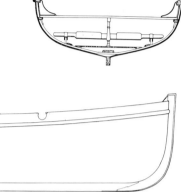

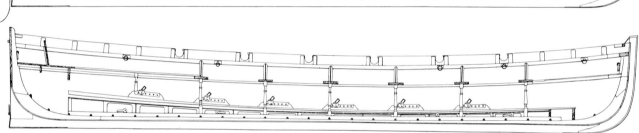

F5 4.5-METRE DINGHY (1/50 scale)
Length between perpendiculars –
4.50m (14ft 9in)
Registered breadth – 1.64m (5ft 5in)
Moulded breadth – 1.60m (5ft 3in)
Depth – 0.65m (2ft 2in)

F5

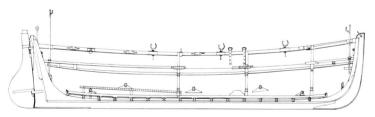

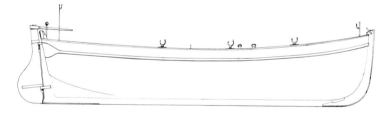

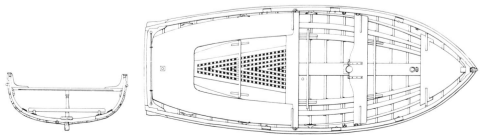

F6 **3.83-METRE UNSINKABLE ROWING DINGHY (1/50 scale)**
Length between perpendiculars –
3.83m (12ft 7in)
Registered breadth – 1.38m (4ft 6in)
Depth – 0.50m (1ft 8in)

F7 **CARLEY FLOAT (LIFERAFT; 1/100 scale)**

F6

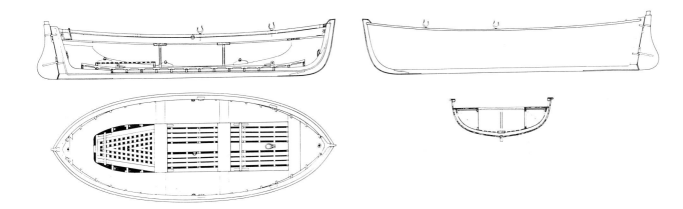

F7

G Armament

G1 ARMAMENT LAYOUT

G1/1 Before June 1940 (1/800 scale)
*Angle of depression varied according to the bearing of the mounting

G1/1

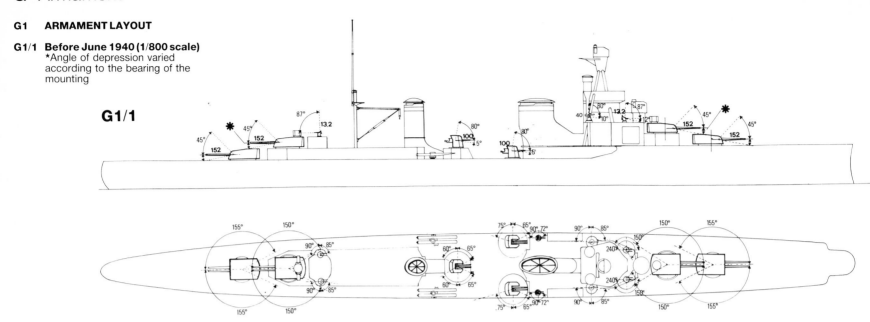

G1/2 From June 1940 (1/800 scale)
* Angle of depression varied according to the bearing of the mounting

G1/2

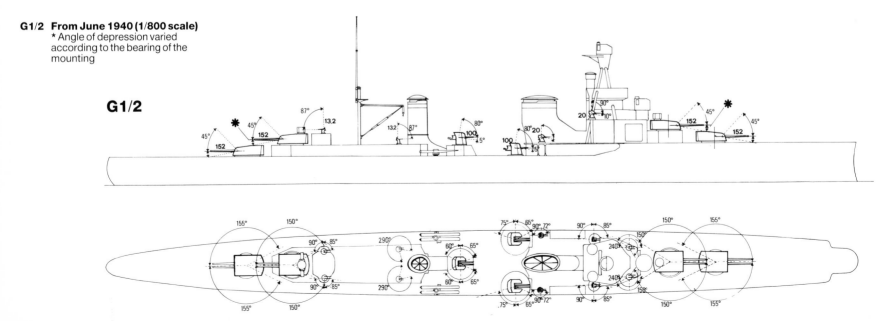

G1/3

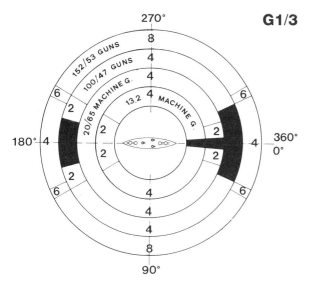

270°

152/53 GUNS
100/47 GUNS
20/65 MACHINE G.
13.2 MACHINE G.

180° 360°
0°

90°

G1/3 Arcs of fire (no scale)

G2/3 Construction of gunhouse (1/50 scale)
1 Longitudinal section
2 Plan view
3 Horizontal section
4 Transverse section
5 Armour plate joints (asterisks refer to figure 1; not to scale)

G2/3

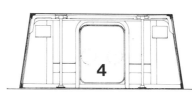

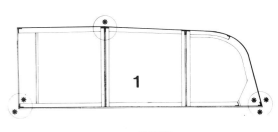

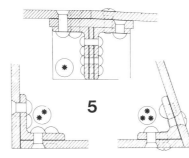

4

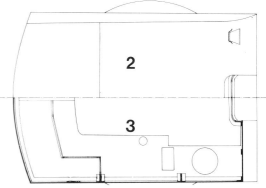

1

2

3

5

G2 152mm/53 ANSALDO M1926 MEDIUM GUN

G2/1 Barrel profile (1/50 scale)

G2/1

630 mm. 525 mm. 410 mm. 282 mm.

8540 mm.

G2/2 Longitudinal sections of barrel (1/25 scale)
1 Breech block housing
2 Cartridge chamber
3 Chase
4 Swell

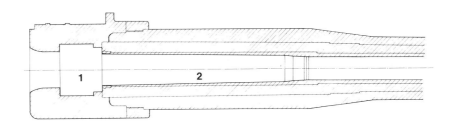

1

2

G2/2

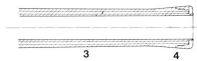

3 4

G Armament

G2/4 Profile section of mounting (actually the similar OTO mounting to later classes; no scale)
By courtesy of Associazione Navimodellisti Bolognesi

G2/4

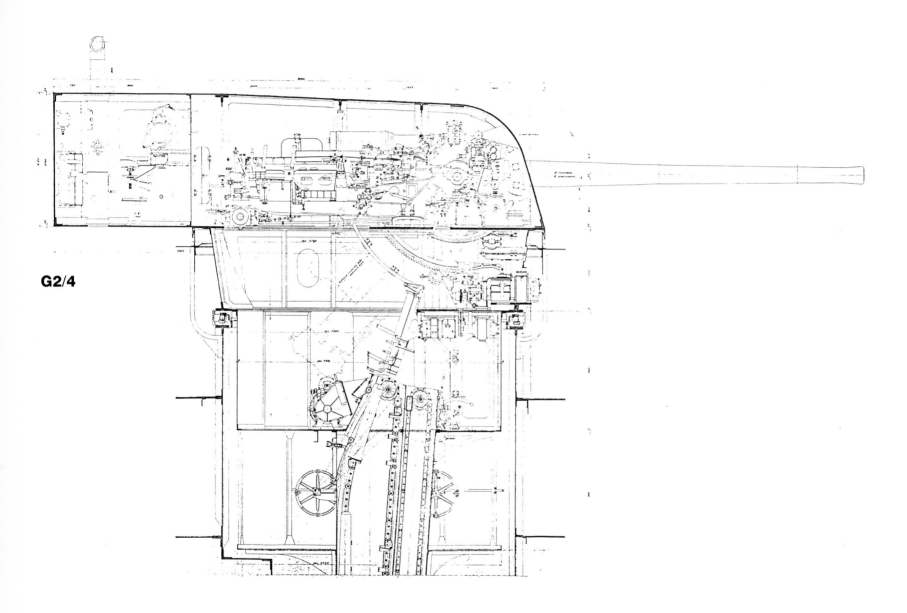

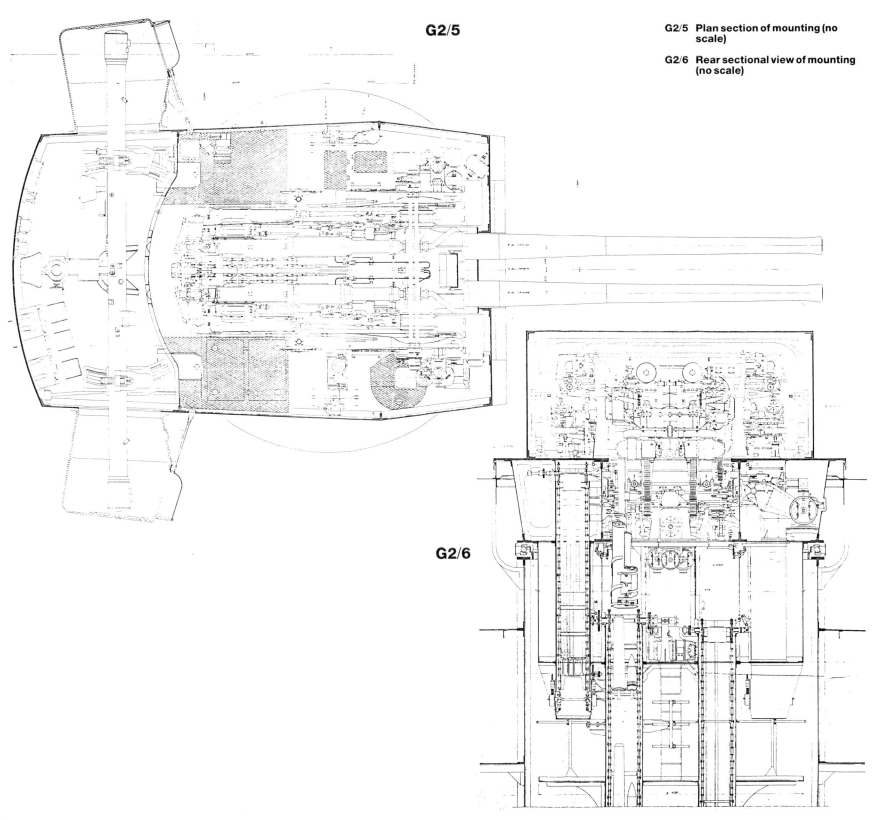

G2/5

G2/5 Plan section of mounting (no scale)

G2/6 Rear sectional view of mounting (no scale)

G2/6

101

G Armament

G3 **100mm/47 OTO M1928 DUAL PURPOSE GUN**

G3/1 Elevation (1/50 scale)

G3/2 Profile inside shield (1/50 scale)

G3/3 Rear view (1/50 scale)

G3/4 Front view inside shield (1/50 scale)

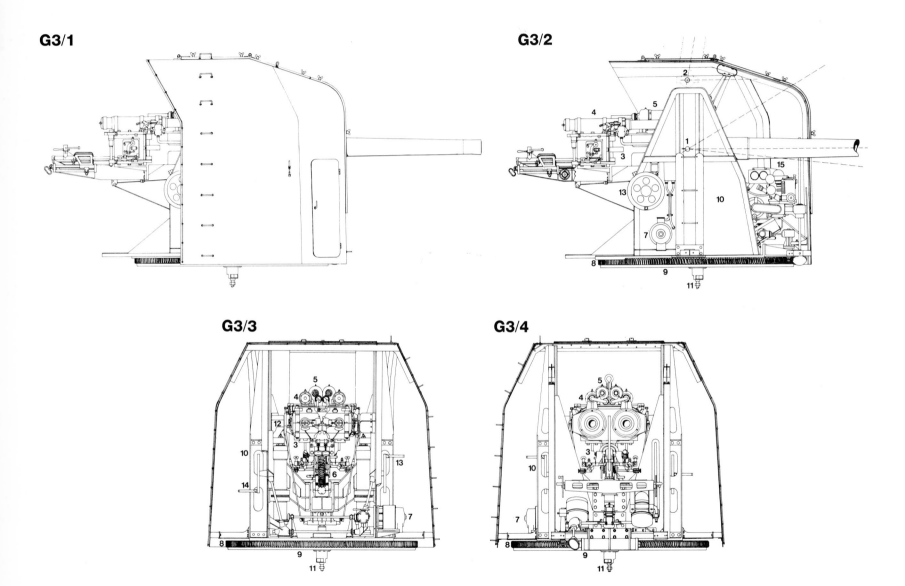

G3/5

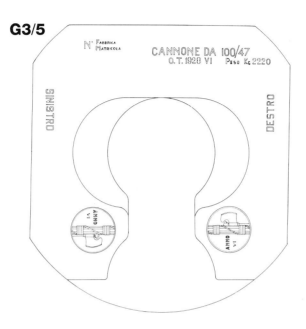

N° Fabbrica Matricola

CANNONE DA 100/47
O.T. 1928 VI   Peso Kg 2220

SINISTRO   DESTRO

AMMO VI   AMMO VI

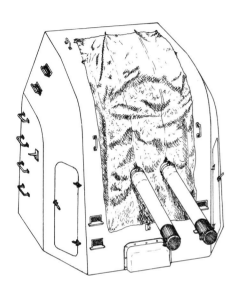

G3/5   Breech markings (1/5 scale)

1 Low trunnion position for surface fire
2 High trunnion position for anti-aircraft fire
3 Cradle
4 Recoil cylinder
5 Recuperator cylinder
6 Elevation mechanism
7 Electric engine for training
8 Rack and pinion training gear
9 Baseplate
10 Trunnion bracket
11 Spindle
12 Trunnion bearing
13 Wheel for manual elevation
14 Wheel for manual training
15 Bearing receiver

G3/6

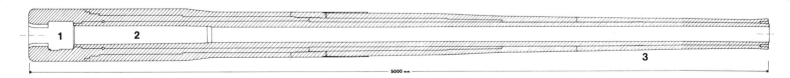

5000 mm

G3/6   Section of barrel (1/25 scale)
1 Breech block
2 Chamber
3 Chase

G Armament

G4 **40mm/39 (2pdr) VICKERS-TERNI AUTOMATIC GUN**

G4/1 Left side elevation (1/25 scale)

G4/2 Plan view (1/25 scale)

G4/3 Rear view (1/25 scale)

G4/4 Right side elevation (1/25 scale)
1. Gunlayer's seat
2. Foot rest
3. Firing pedal
4. Firing transmission rod
5. Elevation wheel
6. Elevation transmission rod
7. Training wheel
8. Training transmission
9. Gun sight
10. Mounting

G4/1

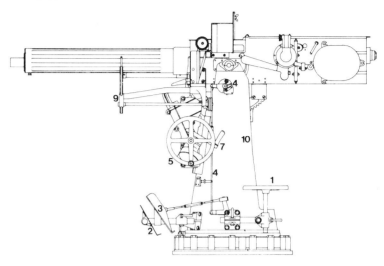

G4/2

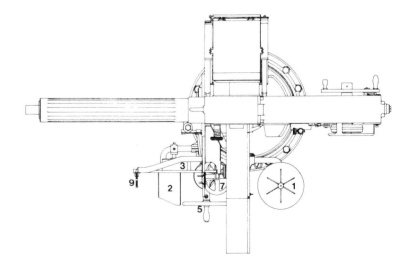

G4/4

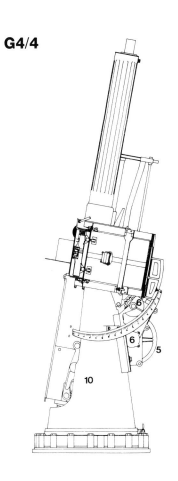

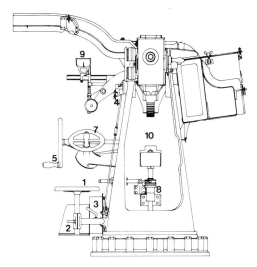

G4/5 **Profile of barrel (1/25 scale)**
1 Trunnion
2 Magazine insert
3 Cooling water filler cap
4 Cooling water discharge cap

G4/6 **Section of barrel (1/12.5 scale)**
1 Firing mechanism
2 Trigger
3 Percussion pin
4 Percussion pin spring
5 Breech and ejector block
6 Safety lever of breech block
7 Cylinder and piston buffer
8 Fuse-setting apparatus
9 Position of cartridge at fuse-setting stage
10 Position of cartridge at firing stage
11 Expended cartridge case
12 Cartridge case ejection
13 Barrel return spring
14 Cooling jacket

G4/5

G4/6

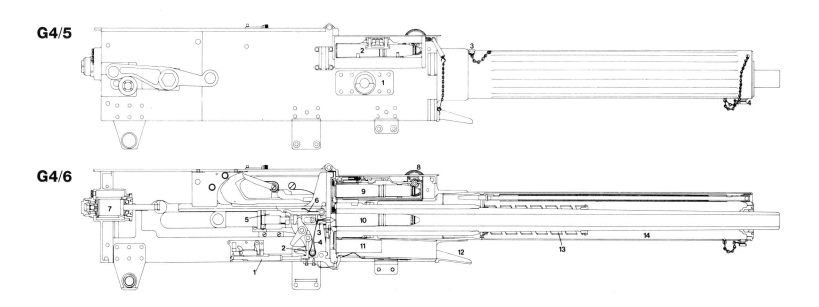

G5/3

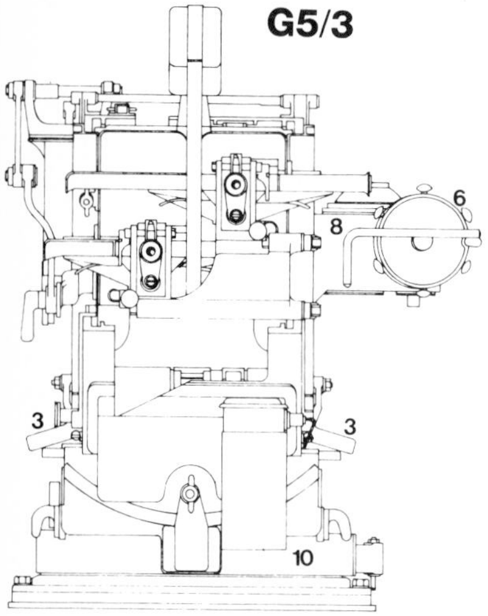

G5/1

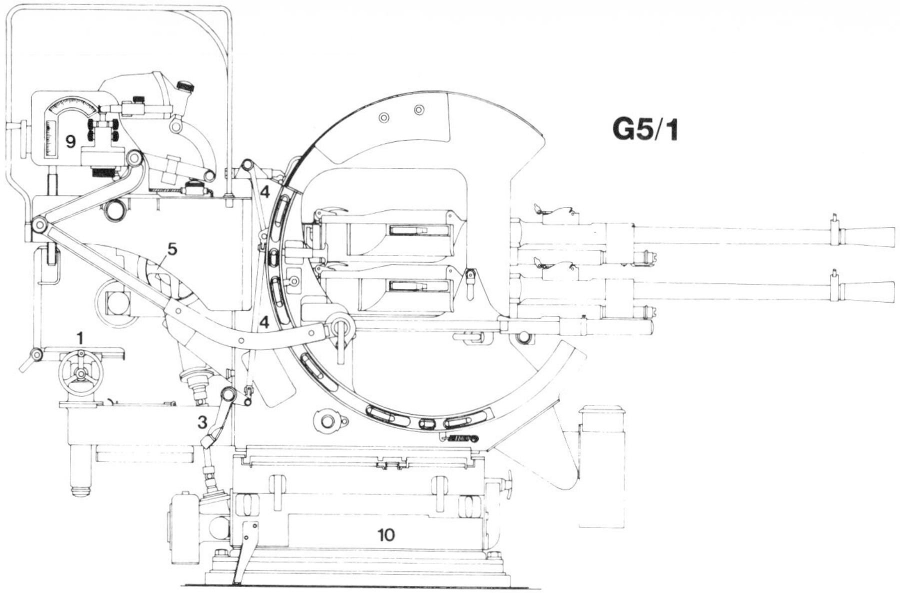

G5/4

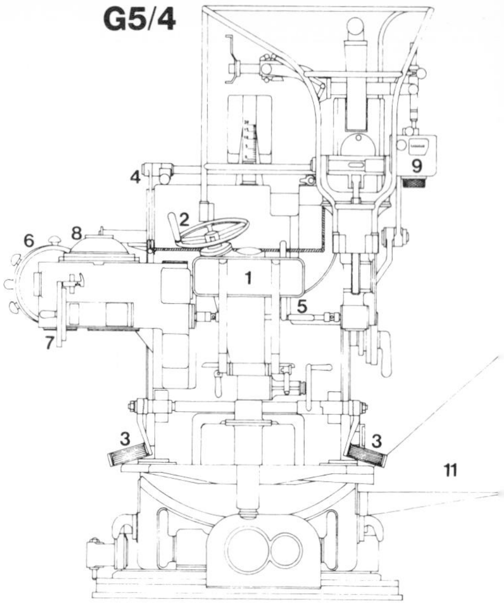

G5/2

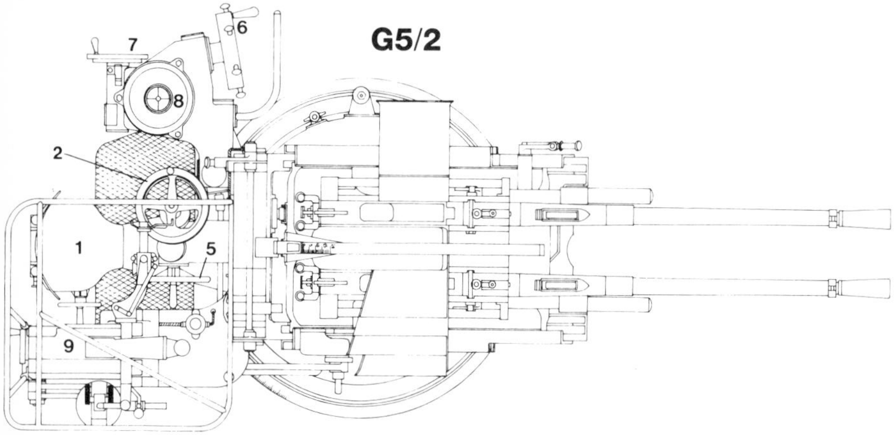

G5/5

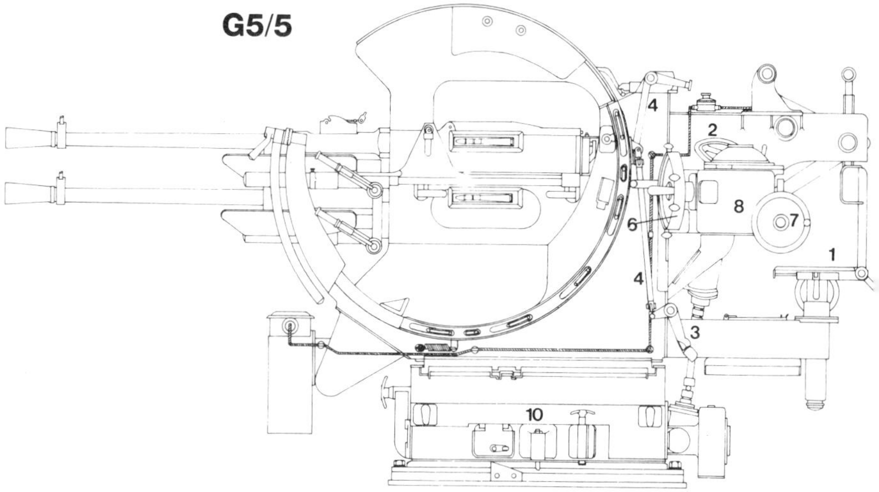

G5/10

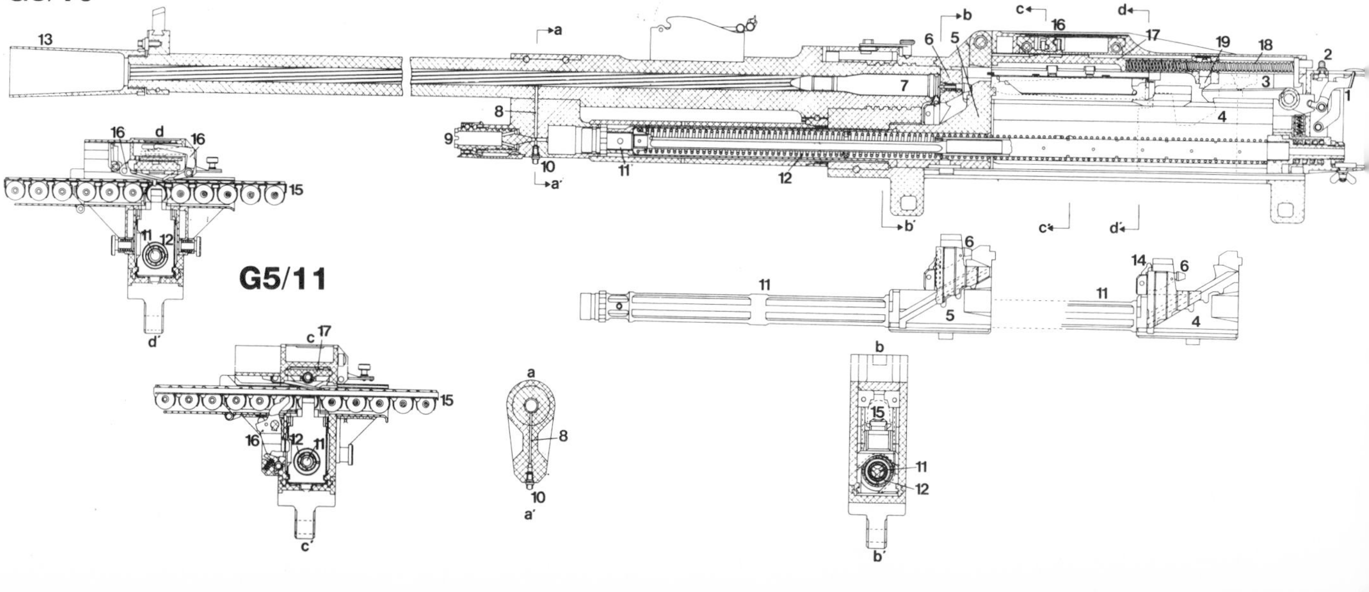

G5	**20mm/65 BREDA MACHINE GUN**
G5/1	**Right side profile (1/25 scale)**
G5/2	**Plan view (1/25 scale)**
G5/3	**Front view (1/25 scale)**
G5/4	**Rear view (1/25 scale)**
G5/5	**Left side profile (1/25 scale)**
1	Adjustable gunlayers' seat
2	Training wheel
3	Firing pedal
4	Fire transmission
5	Elevation wheel
6	Prestabilisation wheel
7	Anti-roll wheel
8	Prestabilisation apparatus pendulum
9	Elevation calculator
10	Platform
11	Expended magazine bin

G5/11

106

G5/6

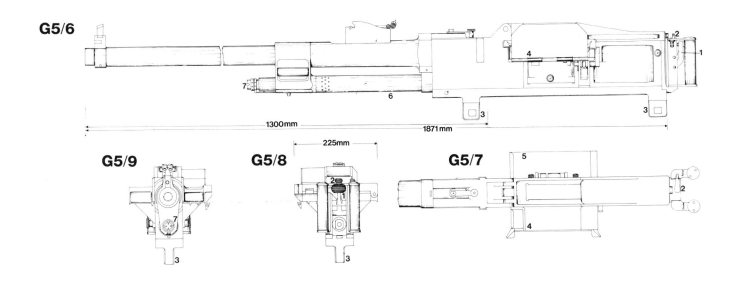

1300mm

1871mm

225mm

G5/9

G5/8

G5/7

G5/6 **Barrel profile (1/10 scale)**

G5/7 **Plan view of barrel (1/10 scale)**

G5/8 **Rear view of barrel (1/10 scale)**

G5/9 **Front view of barrel (1/10 scale)**
1 Trigger
2 Safety catch
3 Mounting fixing lug
4 Magazine insert
5 Magazine ejection
6 Cylinder cover for gas piston
7 Adjustable gas inlet valve

G5/10 **Section of barrel (1/10 scale)**

G5/11 **Transverse section (1/10 scale)**
1 Trigger
2 Safety catch
3 Toothed lever for release of breech block
4 Breech block in open position
5 Breech block in closed position
6 Percussion pin
7 Cartridge in firing position
8 Gas inlet
9 Adjustable gas inlet valve
10 Safety valve
11 Gas piston for opening breech block
12 Gas piston return spring
13 Flash eliminator
14 Cartridge case engaging teeth
15 Magazine
16 Magazine advance lever
17 Magazine advance bar
18 Bar return spring
19 Engaging teeth of the bar with breech block in rear

G6 **13.2mm/75.7 BREDA MACHINE GUN (1/25 scale)**

G6/1 **Right side view**

G6/2 **Plan view**

G6/3 **Longitudinal section**
1 Stabiliser attachment plate
2 Adjustable gunlayer's seat
3 Foot rest
4 Firing pedal
5 Training wheel
6 Elevation wheel
7 Spring of firing mechanism
8 Base
9 Pedestal
10 Rack and pinion gear for training
11 Journal and shaft bearing
12 Elevation gear box
13 Elevation transmission
14 Spindle of elevating arc
15 Transmission link of elevation toe cradle
16 Elevation counterweight
17 Worm of training gear
18 Firing rod
19 Firing transmission system
20 Deflection sight
21 Parallelogram gear

G6/1

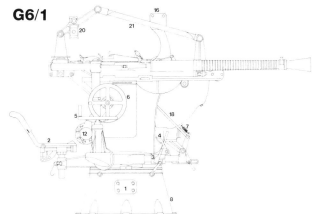

G6/2

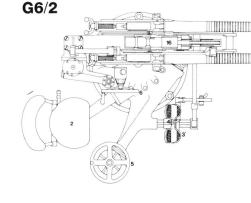

G6/3

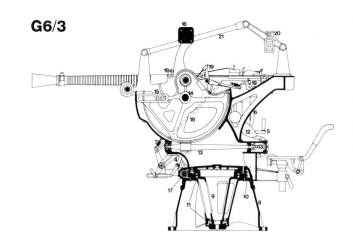

107

G Armament

G7/1

1

2

G7/2

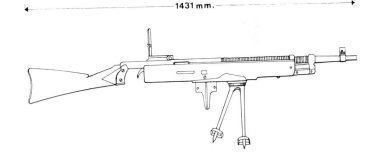

G7/3

G7	**TYPICAL SMALL ARMS (no scale)**
G7/1	**Mod 91 carbine**
1	Gun
2	Bayonet
G7/2	**6.5mm/1915ri machine gun**
G7/3	**7.62mm Berretta automatic pistol**
G8	**MINES**
G8/1	**Minelaying rails (maximum 169 Bollo or P200 mines or 157 Elia type; 1/400 scale)**
1	Mine loading davit
2	Angle bars to secure mines
G8/2	**AE P200/1936 type mine (no scale)**
	Total weight – 1100kg
	Charge weight – 200kg
	Diameter – 1.070m
	Detonating pressure – 280kg
	Number of horns – 9
	Max operating depth – 800m
1	Mine
2	Sinker
3	Hertz horn (detonator)

G8/1

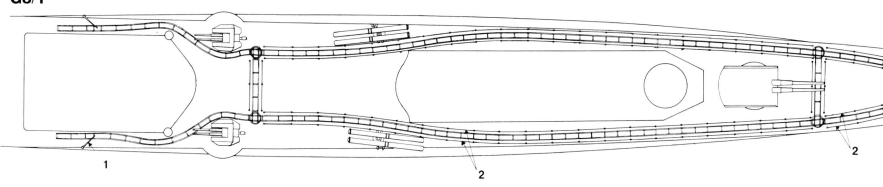

1

2

2

G8/2

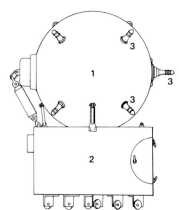

G8/3

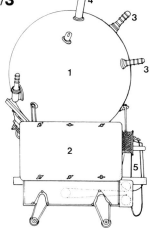

G8/4

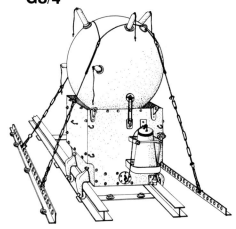

8/3	**AE 145/1925 Elia type mine (no scale)**
	Total weight – 763kg
	Charge weight – 145kg
	Diameter – 965mm
	Detonating pressure – 177kg
	Number of horns – 7
	Max operating depth – 360m
1	Mine
2	Sinker
3	Hertz horn (detonator)
4	Detonator cap
G8/4	**Perspective of P200 and sinker (no scale)**

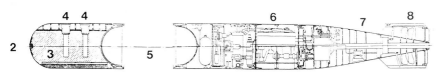

G9/1 SI (Silurificio Italiano) 250/533.4
× 7.5 type A and B, 1929

G9/1

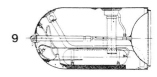

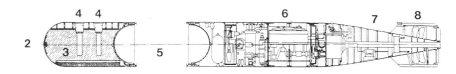

G9/2 SI 250/533.4 × 7.5 type C, 1930

1 Profile (7.5m length)
2 Warhead
3 Charge (270kg TNT)
4 Fuse
5 Compressed air tank
6 Engine compartment
7 Tail
8 Rudders and propellers
9 Practice warhead
10 Torpedo guidance compartment
11 Depth and course regulators

G9/2

G10/1

G10 PARAVANE GEAR

B10/1 Paravane handling gear,
elevation (1/400 scale)

G10/2 Paravane handling gear, plan
view (1/400 scale)

G10/3 Paravane (1/50 scale)
1 Paravanes
2 Paravane davit
Tackle
4 Chains to stream the paravanes
5 Capstans

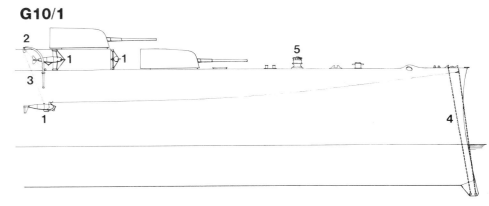

G10/2

G10/3

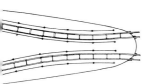

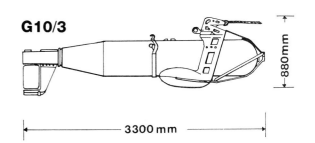

3300 mm

880mm

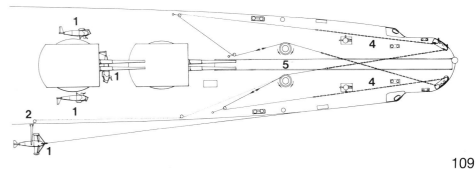

H Ammunition

H1   **AFTER MAGAZINE LAYOUT**
(1/100 scale)

H1/1 **Plan view**

H1/2 **Longitudinal section on**
centreline

H1/2

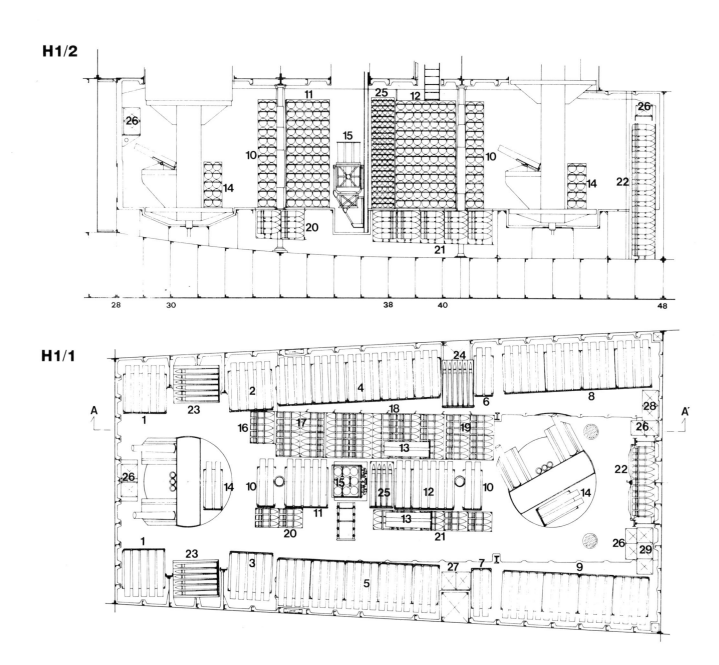

H1/3 Longitudinal section at 'A–A'

H1/4 Transverse section at frame 29

H1/5 Transverse section at frame 38

H1/6 Transverse section at frame 40

H1/7 Transverse section at frame 47

1 Two racks for 45 152mm cartridge cases
2 One rack for 50 152mm cartridge cases
3 One rack for 55 152mm cartridge cases
4 One rack for 114 152mm cartridge cases
5 One rack for 133 152mm cartridge cases
6 One rack for 12 152mm cartridge cases
7 One rack for 14 152mm cartridge cases
8 One rack for 94 152mm cartridge cases
9 One rack for 111 152mm cartridge cases
10 Two racks for 24 152mm cartridge cases
11 One rack for 60 152mm cartridge cases
12 One rack for 84 152mm cartridge cases
13 Two sliding racks for 24 152mm cartridge cases
14 Two racks for 10 152mm cartridge cases
15 One cage-type hoist for 9 152mm cartridge cases
16 Bin for 15 152mm shells
17 Bin for 96 152mm shells
18 Bin for 152 152mm shells
19 Bin for 115 152mm shells
20 Bin for 25 152mm shells
21 Bin for 65 152mm shells
22 Bin for 242 152mm shells
23 Two racks for 90 100mm shells
24 One rack for 60 100mm shells
25 One rack for 80 100mm shells
26 Five racks for 6 boxes of 80 20mm cartridges
27 One rack for 10 boxes of 20mm cartridges
28 One rack for 12 boxes of 20mm cartridges
29 One rack for 16 boxes of 20mm cartridges
30 Two boxes of 100 25mm magazines
Total ammunition
942 152mm cartridge cases
710 152mm shells
320 100m shells
5440 20mm cartridges
2000 25mm magazines

H1/3

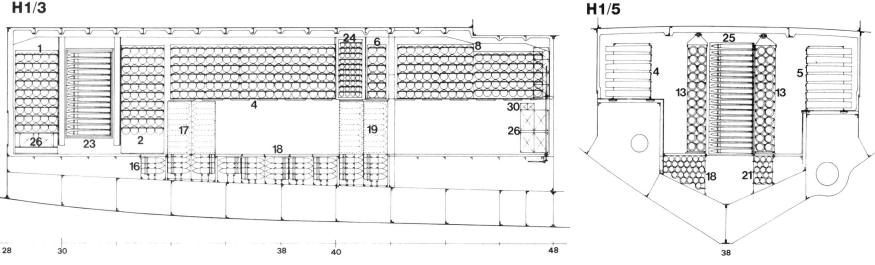

H1/5

H1/4

H1/6

H1/7

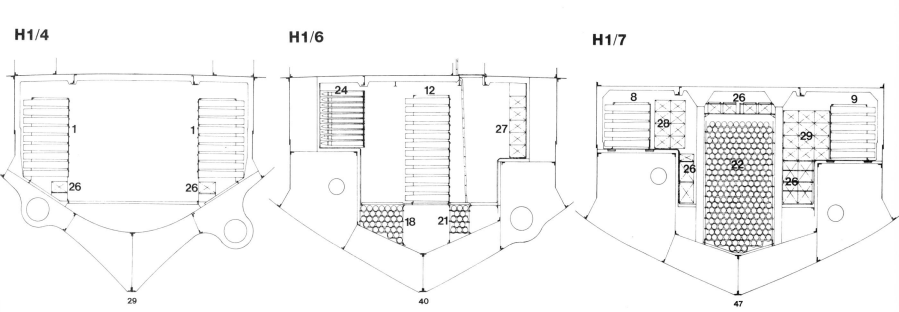

H Ammunition

H2/1

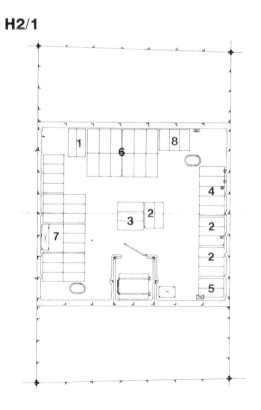

H2/2

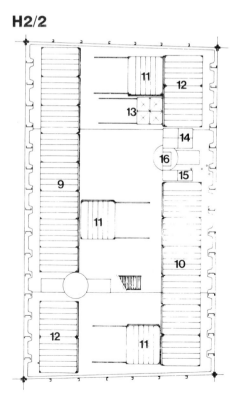

H2/3

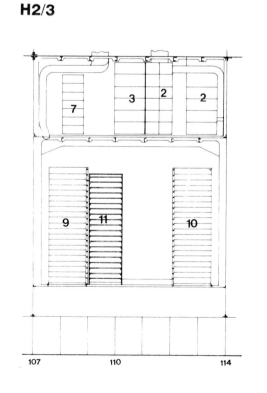

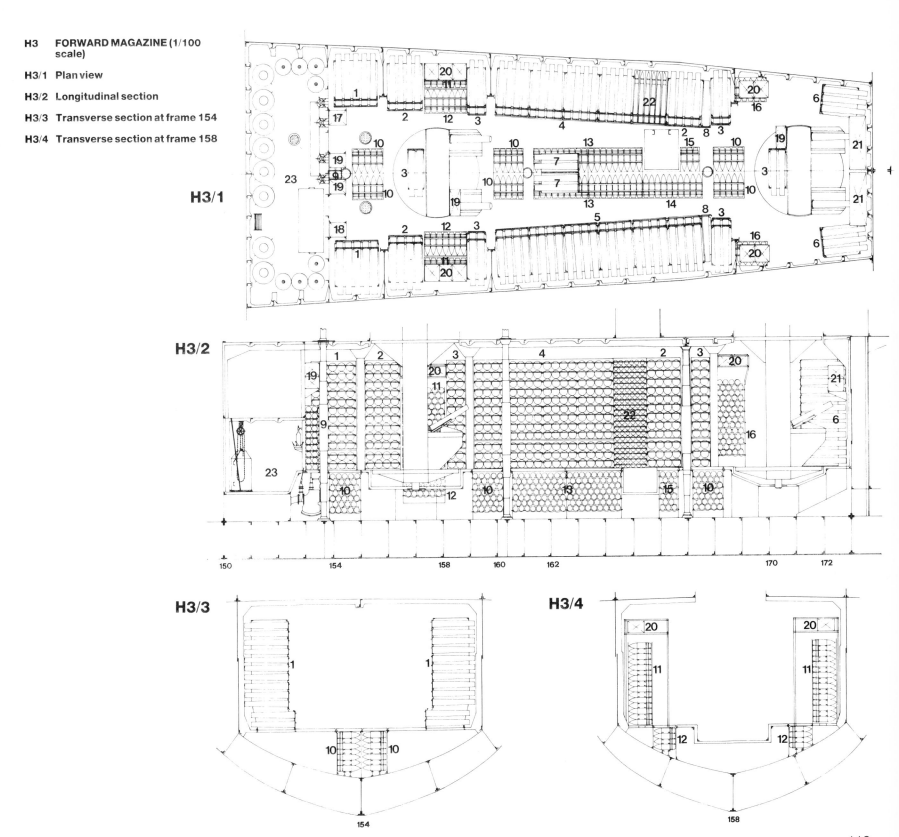

H3 FORWARD MAGAZINE (1/100 scale)

H3/1 Plan view

H3/2 Longitudinal section

H3/3 Transverse section at frame 154

H3/4 Transverse section at frame 158

H3/1

H3/2

H3/3

H3/4

113

H4/1

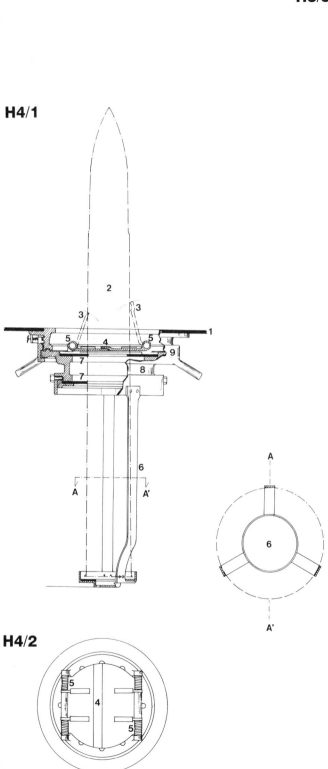

H3/5

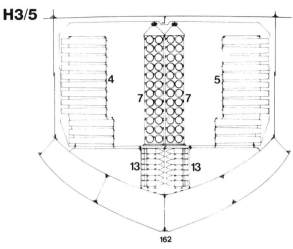

162

H3/6

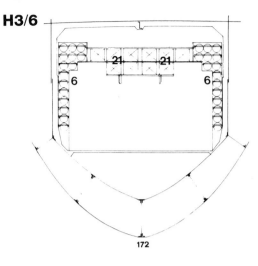

172

H4/2

H4/4

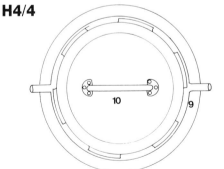

H4/3

H3/5 Transverse section at frame 162

H3/6 Transverse section at frame 172

1	Two racks for 60 152mm cartridge cases
2	Three racks for 48 152mm cartridge cases
3	Six racks for 24 152mm cartridge cases
4	One rack for 192 152mm cartridge cases
5	One rack for 288 152mm cartridge cases
6	Two racks for 15 152mm cartridge cases
7	Two sliding racks for 24 152mm cartridge cases
8	Two racks for 7 152mm cartridge cases

9	One bin for 20 152mm shells
10	Six bins for 32 152mm shells
11	Two bins for 98 152mm shells
12	Two bins for 26 152mm shells
13	Two bins for 120 152mm shells
14	One bin for 66 152mm shells
15	One bin for 18 152mm shells
16	Two bins for 58 152mm shells
16	One rack for 2 boxes of 80 20mm cartridges
18	One rack for 4 boxes of 80 20mm cartridges
19	Four racks for 3 boxes of 80 20mm cartridges
20	Four racks for 4 boxes of 80 20mm cartridges
21	Two racks for 10 boxes of 80 20mm cartridges
22	One rack for 120 100mm shells
23	Store for 8 torpedo warheads

Total ammunition
980 152mm cartridge cases
900 152mm shells
120 100mm shells
4320 20mm cartridges
8 torpedo warheads

H4 GAS-PROOF 100mm AMMUNITION SCUTTLE (1/12.5 scale)

H4/1 Longitudinal section

H4/2 Plan view

H4/3 Scuttle closing port in position, longitudinal section

H4/4 Scuttle closing port in position, longitudinal section

1	Upper deck
2	Shell in raised position
3	Covers in open position
4	Covers in closed position
5	Torsion spring
6	Shell hoist cage
7	Rubber packing
8	Cage ring with mortised flange
9	Mortise ring
10	Closing port with mortised flange

H5   **152mm SHELLS (1/10 scale)**

H5/1 **Armour piercing (one charge weight 46.765kg)**
1   'Silumin' windshield or ballistic cap
2   Cap
3   Shell
4   Centring band
5   Driving band
6   Fuse
7   Detonator
8   Charge

H5/2 **High explosive (one charge weight 39.940kg)**
1   'Silumin' ballistic cap
2   Nose fuse
3   Shell
4   Centring band
5   Driving band
6   Charge

H5/3 **Starshell**
1   Ballistic cap
2   Fuse
3   Shell
4   Centring band
5   Driving band
6   Charge

H5/1

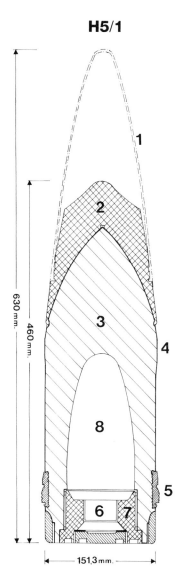

H5/2

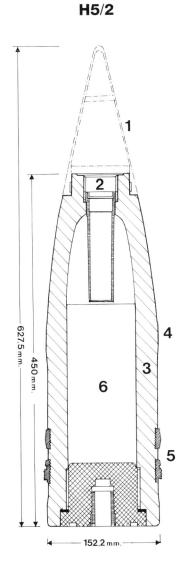

H5/3

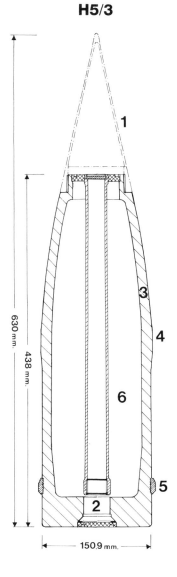

115

H Ammunition

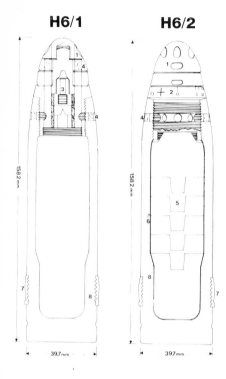

H6/1   **H6/2**

158.2 mm

39.7 mm

H6   **40mm (2 pdr) SHELL (1/2 scale)**

H6/1   **Section without explosive charge**

H6/2   **Section with charge**
1   Fuse-setting mechanism
2   Graduation scale
3   Time fuse
4   Cork
5   Explosive charge
6   Paper tube
7   Driving band
8   External case

H7   **13.2mm CARTRIDGES (1/2 scale)**   **H7/2**   **SIT tracer round**

H7/1   **External view**   **H7/3**   **Armour piercing round**
1   Profile
2   Base (the positions 1, 2 and 3 were   **H7/4**   **Common round**
     inscribed with the manufacturer, date
     and tester's initials respectively)   **H7/5**   **Improved tracer round**
     Types were identified as follows: 1   Brass cartridge case
     Tracer – blue cap, metallic projectile   2   Percussion cap
     Armour piercing – metallic cap, white   3   Propellant charge
     projectile   4   Steel shell case
     Common – metallic cap and projectile   5   SI charge (tracer)
     Improved tracer – metallic cap and   6   Tracer cartridge case
     red projectile   7   Tracer mixture
         8   Fuse
         9   Lead cap
         10   Ballistic cap
         11   Iron shell

H7/1

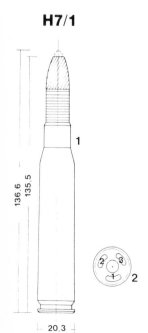

136.6

135.5

20.3

H7/2

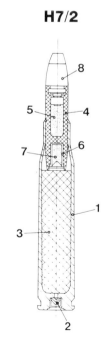

H7/3

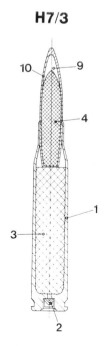

H7/4

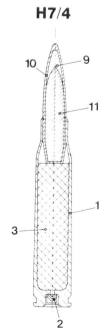

H7/5

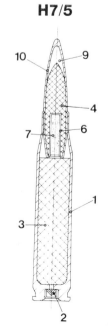

I Fire control

I1

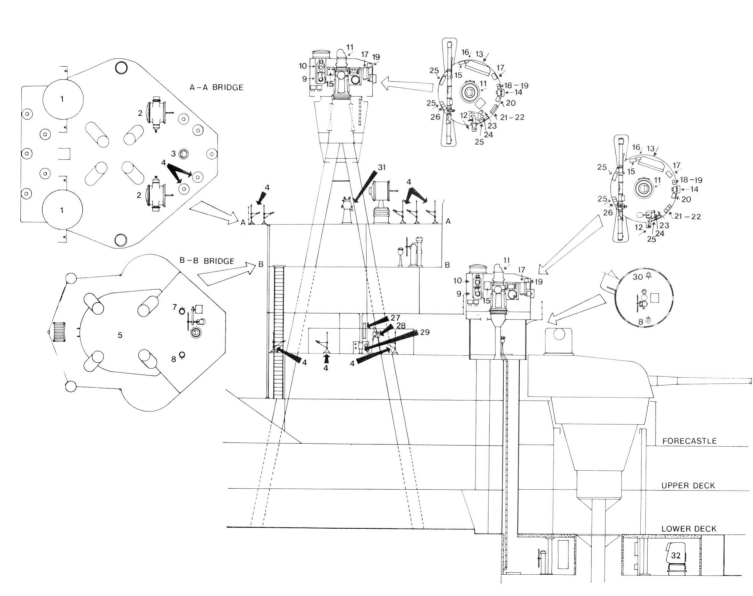

I Fire control

I2/2

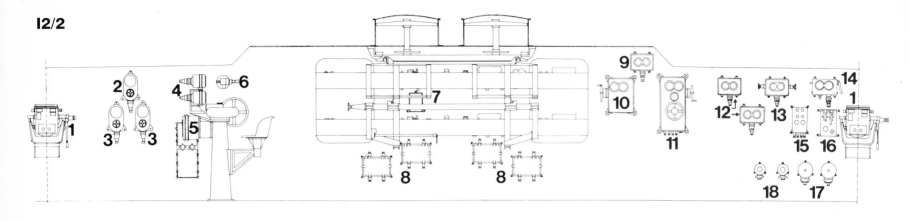

I2/1

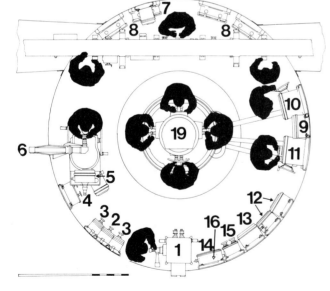

I2 **MAIN ARMAMENT DIRECTOR**
(1/50 scale)

I2/2 **Plan of equipment layout**

I2/2 **Linear profile of equipment**
1 Inclinometer
2 Order receiver
3 Order transmitter
4 Training receiver
5 Training transmitter
6 Searcher for error finder
7 Auxiliary range receiver
8 Junction box
9 Course and speed of target receiver
10 Deflection box
11 Sight box
12 Range receiver
13 Course and speed of target
transmitter
14 Spotting transmitter
15 'Guns ready' lamp board
16 Consent for automatic range
reduction (for 'ladder' firing)
17 Alarm bells
18 Klaxon
19 Director control gear

I3 **FIRE CONTROL SIGHT**
(perspective view; no scale)
This is the APG (*Apparato Punteria
Generali*) described in the Fire
Control section of the Introduction

I3

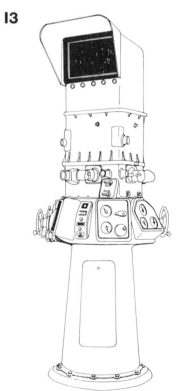

J1

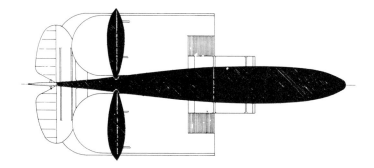

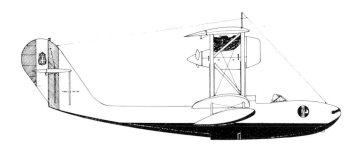

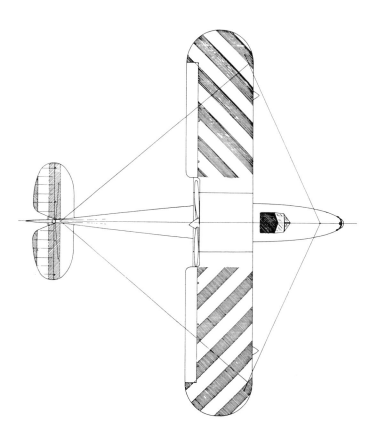

J1 **'CRDA' CANT 25 AR FLYING BOAT (1/100 scale)**
Colour scheme
Upper surface – white or aluminium
Lower surface – white or aluminium
Fuselage – white or aluminium
Fuselage underwater surface – black
Floats, lower surface – black
Wing stripes – red
Fuselage insignia – Fasces on blue ground
Rudder – green, white and red, plus Savoia's shield
Stabiliser upper surface – green white and red

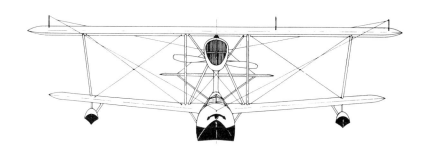

J2 'IMAM' RO–43 Mk I FLOATPLANE (1/100 scale)

Colour scheme

Upper surfaces – white or aluminium
Lower surfaces – white or aluminium
Fuselage – white or aluminium
Floats, lower surface – black
Wing stripes – red
National insignia – black
Lateral insignia – Fasces on blue ground
Until June 1940 identification code: ship name in black and number of the aircraft (1 or 2) in red; rudder green, white and red plus Savoia's shield.
From June 1940 identification code: number of naval division in black, plus number of ship in black, plus number of the aircraft in red; rudder white cross on black ground plus Savoia's shield

J2

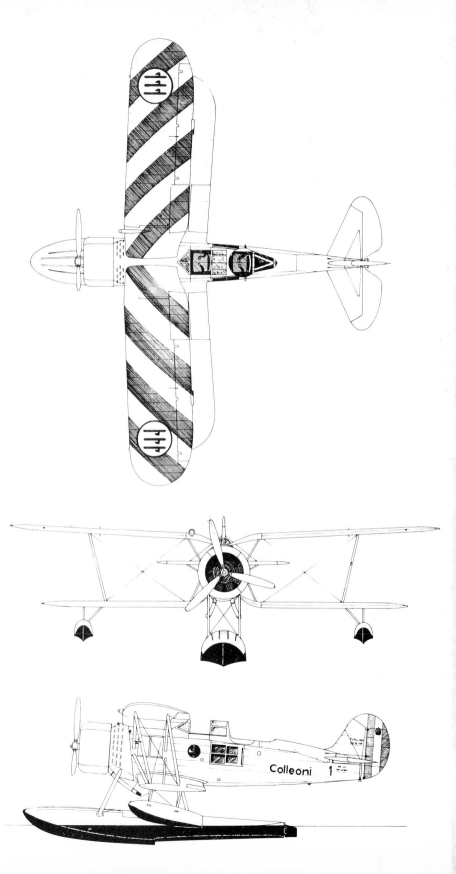

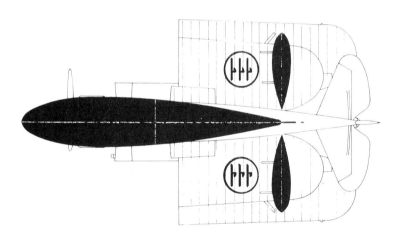

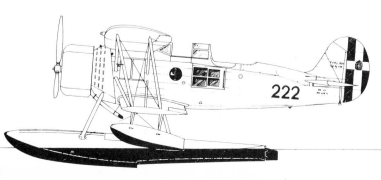